KNOCK 'EM DEAD

With Great Answers to Tough Interview Questions

KNOCK 'EM DEAD

With Great Answers to Tough Interview Questions

MARTIN JOHN YATE

BOB ADAMS, INC.
PUBLISHERS
Holbrook, Massachusetts

Acknowledgments

My thanks to the following people who in different ways have helped this book become what it is today—the only internationally published job-hunting guide of its kind.

From the employment services world: Dunhill Personnel System presidents—Brad Brin of Milwaukee, Warren Mahan of Maine, Leo Salzman of Columbus, Dave Bontempo of Southhampton, Paul and Pat Erickson of Shawnee Mission, Jim Fowler of Huntsville (and Ray Johnson), Stan Hart of Troy, Mike Badgett of Cherry Hills Village, and John Webb and everyone in beautiful San Antonio.

Thanks also to Don Kipper of Ernst & Whinney, Dan O'Brien of Grumman Aerospace, Amy Marglis and Kathy Seich of Merrill Lynch, Roger Villanueva of I.M.S., Victor Lindquist of Northwestern University, Ed Fitzpatrick of the University of Michigan, and Mary Giannini of Columbia University.

Gratitude is due to Eric Blume for his editorial assistance in the first three editions, and to my new editor, Brandon Toropov. Thanks go also to that man of vision, my publisher Bob Adams, and the people who got this hot little book into your hands—the tireless sales representatives of Bob Adams, Inc. And special thanks to Jill, for being the brightest star in my firmament.

Published by
Bob Adams, Inc.
260 Center Street
Holbrook, Massachusetts 02343

ISBN: 1-55850-875-9
ISBN: 1-55850-864-3 (paperback)

Manufactured in the United States of America.
A B C D E F G H I J
A B C D E F G H I J (hardcover)

Contents

Dedication

To your successful job hunt.

Introduction

Why another book about interviewing? Because the others stop at that critical point when the tough questions start flying. They lack the practical advice of what to do in the heat of battle. *Knock 'em Dead* will first help you to arrange the interview and then will get right to the heart of your greatest interview dread: "How on earth do I answer that one?" It takes command where others admit defeat.

Here, you'll get hundreds of the tough, sneaky, mean and low-down questions that interviewers love to throw at you. With each question, I will show you what the interviewer wants to find out about you, and explain how you should reply. After each explanation, you'll get a sample answer and suggestions on how to customize it to your individual circumstances. The examples themselves come from real life, things people like you have done on the job that got them noticed. I'll show you how they packaged those experiences—how they used their practical experience to turn a job interview into a job offer.

Perhaps you are trying to land your first job or are returning to the workplace. Maybe you are a seasoned executive taking another step up the ladder of success. Whoever you are, this book will help you, because it shows you how to master any interview and succeed with any interviewer. You will learn that every interviewer tries to evaluate each candidate by the same three criteria: Is the candidate *able* to do the job? Is he or she *willing* to put in the effort to make the job a success? And last but not least, is he or she *manageable*? You will learn how to demonstrate your superiority in each of these areas, under all interview conditions.

The job interview is a measured and ritualistic mating dance in which the best partners whirl away with the glittering prizes. The steps of this dance are the give-and-take, question-and-response exchanges that make meaningful business conversation. Learn the steps and you, too, can dance the dance.

Your partner in the dance, obviously, is the interviewer, who will lead with tough questions that carry subtleties hidden from the untrained ear. You will learn how to recognize those questions-within-questions. And with this knowledge, you will be cool, calm, and collected, while other candidates are falling apart with attacks of interview nerves.

How do you discover hidden meanings in questions? I recently heard a story about a young woman who was doing very well on an interview for a high-pressure job in a television studio. The interviewer wanted to know how she would react in the sudden, stressful situations common in TV, and got his answer when he said, "You know, I don't really think you're suitable for the job. Wouldn't you be better off in another company?" With wounded pride, the job-hunter stormed out in a huff. She never knew how close she was, how easy it would have been to land the job. The interviewer smiled: He had caught her with a tough question. Did the interviewer mean what he said? What was really behind the question? How could she have handled it and landed the job? The great answers to tough questions like that and many others are waiting for you in the following pages.

The job interview has many similarities to good social conversation. Job offers always go to the interviewee who can turn a one-sided examination of skills into a dynamic exchange between two professionals. In *Knock 'em Dead*, you will learn the techniques for exciting and holding your interviewer's attention, and at the same time, for promoting yourself as the best candidate for the job.

This book will carry you successfully through the worst interviews you could ever face. It is written in four interconnected parts. "The Well-Stocked Briefcase" gets you ready for the fray. You will quickly learn to build a resume with broad appeal and to use a unique customizing technique guaranteed to make your application stand out as something special. You will also learn how to tap into thousands of job openings at all levels that never reach the newspapers.

Once you are ready for action, "Getting to Square One" examines all the approaches to getting job interviews and teaches you simple and effective ways to set up multiple interviews. This section ends with techniques to steer you successfully through those increasingly common telephone screening interviews.

"Great Answers to Tough Interview Questions" gives you just that, and teaches you some valuable business lessons that will contribute to your future success. All successful companies look for the same things in their employees, and everything they're looking for you either have or can develop. Sound impossible? I will show you the 20 key personality traits that can convey your potential for success to any interviewer.

"Finishing Touches" assures that out-of-sight-out-of-mind will not apply to you after you leave the interviewer's office. You will even discover how to get a job offer after you have been turned down for the position, and how to negotiate the best salary and package for yourself when a job offer is made. Most important, the sum of those techniques will give you tremendous self-confidence when you go to an interview: No more jitters, no more sweaty palms.

If you want to know how business works and what savvy businesspeople look for in an employee, if you want to discover how to land the interview and then conquer the interviewer, this book is for you. *Knock 'em Dead* delivers what you need to win the job of your dreams. Now get to it, step ahead in your career, and knock 'em dead.

Martin John Yate
New York

I

The Well-Stocked Briefcase

Have you heard the one about the poor man who wanted to become a famous bear-slayer? Once upon a time, in a town plagued by bears, lived a man. The man had always wanted to travel but had neither the right job nor the money. If he could kill a bear, then he could travel to other places plagued with bears and make his living as a bear-slayer. Every day he sat on the porch and waited for a bear to come by. After many weeks of waiting, he thought he might go looking for bears. He didn't know much about them, except that they were out there.

Full of hope, he rose before dawn, loaded his single-shot musket, and headed for the forest. On reaching the edge of the forest, he raised the musket and fired into the dense undergrowth.

Do you think he hit a bear or, for that matter, anything else? Why was he bear-hunting with a single-shot musket and why did he shoot before seeing a bear? What was his problem? Our hero couldn't tell dreams from reality. He went hunting unprepared and earned what he deserved. The moral of the tale is this: When you look for a job, keep a grip on reality, go loaded for bear, and don't go off half-cocked.

Out there in the forest of your profession hide many companies and countless opportunities. These are major corporations, small family-affairs, and some in between. They all have something in common, and that's problems. To solve those problems, companies need people. *Anyone hired for any job is a problem-solver.* Think about your present job function: What problems would occur if you weren't there? You were hired to take care of those problems.

Being a problem-solver is good, but companies prefer to hire and promote someone who also understands what business is all about. There are three lessons you should remember on this score.

Lesson One: Companies are in business to make money. People have loyalty to companies; companies have loyalty only to the bottom line. They make money by being economical and saving money. They make money by being efficient and saving time. And if they save time, they save money, and have more time to make more money.

Lesson Two: Companies and you are exactly alike. You both want to make as much money as possible in as short a time as possible. That allows you to do the things you really want with the rest of your time.

Lesson Three: There are buyer's markets (advantage: prospective employer) and there are seller's markets (advantage: prospective employee). Job offers put you in a seller's market, and give you the whip hand.

Lesson One tells you the three things every company is interested in. *Lesson Two* says to recognize that you really have the same goals as the company. *Lesson Three* says that anyone with any sense wants to be in a seller's market.

If you look for jobs one at a time, you put yourself in a buyer's market. If you implement my advice in *Knock 'em Dead*, you will have multiple interviews because you'll be able to handle the toughest questions, thereby getting multiple job offers. And job offers, however good or bad they are, will put you in a seller's market, regardless of the economic climate.

Operating in a seller's market requires knowing who, where, and what your buyers are in the market for, then being ready with the properly packaged product.

In this section, you will see how to identify all the companies that could be in need of your services. You will discover names of the president, those on the board, those in management; company sales volume; complete lines of company services or products; and size of the outfit. You will evaluate and package your professional skills in a method guaranteed to have appeal to every employer. And you will discover highly desirable professional skills you never thought you had.

A well-stocked briefcase requires more than looking idly through the want ads. It means a little discipline, a little effort. But aren't your professional goals worth it?

It will take a couple of days' work to get you loaded for bear. Your first action should be a trip to the library (taking sufficient paper and pens). On the way, purchase push-pins, a large-scale area map, and some stick-on labels—and rustle up a three-foot piece of string. Take some sandwiches; there is no feeling in the world like eating lunch on the library steps.

1.
Discovering What's Out There

At the library, walk in purposefully and ask for the reference section. When you find it, wander around for a few minutes before staking a claim. You will discover that libraries are a good place to watch the human race, so get the best seat in the house. Make sure you have a clear view of the librarian's desk. When you need a rest, that's where all the comic relief takes place.

There are a number of reference books you can consult, and they are listed in the "Bibliography." I won't waste space showing you how to use them here—the librarian will be happy to do that.

Your goal is to identify and build personalized dossiers on the companies in your chosen geographic area. Do not be judgmental about what and who they might appear to be—remember, you are fishing for possible job openings, so cast your net wide and list them all.

Take a pad of paper, and using a separate sheet for each company, copy all the relevant company information onto that piece of paper. So that we agree on what's relevant, take a look at the example on page 18.

There, you see the names of the company's president and chairman of the board, a description of the complete lines of company services and products, the size of the company, and the locations of its various branches. Of course, if you find other interesting information, copy it down, by all means. For instance, you might come across information on growth or shrinkage in a particular area of a company; or you might read about recent acquisitions the company has made. Write it all down.

All this information will help you shine at the interview in three different ways. Your knowledge gives the company a favorable impression at the first meeting; the company notices that you made an effort. That no one else bothers

<u>Corporation, Inc.</u>

Headquarters:
123 Main Street
Boston, MA 02127

Main phone: 617/555-1200
Personnel (Joseph Smith, Director): 617/555-1234

President: Richard Johnson (for 3 yrs.)
COB: William Jones (for 2 yrs.)

Director of Word Processing Services: Peter Lee

Company produces a complete line of office machines:
calculators, adding machines, typewriters (electric,
electronic, manual), telephones, computerized
switching systems, and a wide range of peripheral
equipment. Employs 1200, all in Massachusetts.

This location is primarily an administrative
facility, but it provides all services for the firm
(research, repair, operations, <u>word processing</u>).
Manufacturing facilities located in Worcester
(calculators, telephone equipment, peripherals) and
Wakefield (typewriters, computers).

Sales (1985): $334.3 million
Profits: +5% over last 5 years

Recently acquired Disko, Inc. (Braintree, MA), a
software firm (looks like it's diversifying ???).
Maybe has something big in the works (possible merger
with The Bigg Corporation).

to make the effort is a second benefit. And third, the combination says that you respect the company, and therefore, by inference, the interviewer: That helps set you apart from the herd.

All your effort has an obvious short-term value: It helps you win job offers. It also has value in the long term, because you are building a personalized reference work of your industry/specialty/profession that will help you throughout your career whenever you wish to make a job change.

Unfortunately, no reference work is complete. The very size and scope of such works necessitate that most are just a little out of date at publication time. Also, no reference work lists every company. Because you don't know what company has the very best job for you, you need to research as many businesses in your area as possible, and therefore you will have to look through additional reference books.

Be sure to check out any specialized guides mentioned in the "Bibliography," including the *Standard & Poor's Register* and your state's manufacturing directory.

At the end of the day, pack up and head home for some well-deserved troughing and sluicing. Remember to purchase a map of your area, push-pins, and small stick-on labels for implementing the next step of your plan.

Put the map on the wall. Attach the string to a push-pin, stick the pin on the spot where you live, and draw concentric circles at intervals of one mile. In a short space of time, you will have defaced a perfectly good map, but you'll have a physical outline of your job-hunting efforts.

Next, take out the company biographies prepared at the library and write "#1" on the first. Find the firm's location on the map and mark it with a push-pin. Then, mark an adhesive label "#1" and attach it to the head of the pin. As you progress, a dramatic picture of your day's work appears. Each pin-filled circle is a territory that needs to be covered, and each of those pins represents a potential job.

It is likely you will be back at the library again, finishing off this reference work and preparing your resume. The research might take a few days. Try walking to the library the next time. Not only is it cheaper (a sound reason in itself), but the exercise is very important to you. You are engaged in a battle of wits, and the healthier you are physically, the sharper you will be mentally. You need your wits about you, because there are always well qualified people looking for the best jobs.

But remember: It is not the most qualified who always get the job. It is the person who is best prepared that wins every time. Job hunters who knock 'em dead at the interview are those who do the homework and preparation that a failure will not do. Do a little more walking. Do a little more research.

Almost everybody looking for a new job buys the newspaper and then carefully misuses it. A recent story tells of a job hunter who started by waiting for the Sunday paper to be published. He read the paper and circled six jobs. Called the first to find it had already been filled, and in the process, got snubbed by someone whose voice had yet to break, requesting that he write in the future and send a resume. As anything is better than facing telephone conversations like that, the job hunter didn't call the other five companies, but took a week to write a resume that no one would read, let alone understand. Sent it to a dozen companies. Waited a week for someone to call. Waited another week. Kicked the cat. Felt bad about that, worse about himself, and had a couple of drinks. Phone rang, someone was interested in the resume but, unfortunately, not in someone who slurred his words at lunchtime. Felt worse, stayed in bed late. Phone rang: an interview! Felt good, went to the interview. Prospective employer will contact in a few days. They didn't, and in the subsequent panicked calls to them, everybody was mysteriously unavailable. The job hunter began to feel like a blot on God's landscape.

That is obviously an extreme example, but the story is a little too close to the bone for many, and it illustrates the wrong way to use the paper when you're looking for a job.

Unfortunately, most people use either the newspaper or reference books, but rarely both. They run the risk of ending up in the buyer's market. Not a good place to be.

While reference books give you bags of hard information about a company, they tell you little about specific job openings. Newspapers, on the other hand, tell you about specific jobs that need filling now, but give you few hard facts about the company. The two types of research should complement each other. Often you will find ads in the newspaper for companies you have already researched. What a powerful combination of information that gives you going in the door to the interview!

The correct use of newspapers is to identify all companies that are currently hiring. Write down the pertinent details of each particular job opening on a separate piece of paper, as you did earlier with the reference books. Include the company's name, address, phone number, and contact names.

In addition to finding openings that bear your particular title, look for all the companies that regularly hire for your field. The fact that your job is not being advertised does not mean a company is not looking for you; if a company is in a hiring mode, a position for you might be available. In the instances when a company is active but has not been advertising specifically for your skills, write down all relevant company contact data. Such a firm should be contacted: You could be the solution to a problem that has only just arisen; or even one they have despaired of ever solving.

It is always a good idea to examine back issues of the newspaper. They can provide a rich source of job opportunities that remain unfilled from prior advertising efforts.

The reason you must use a combination of reference books and advertisements is that companies tend to hire in cycles. When you rely exclusively on newspapers, you miss those companies just about to start or just ending their hiring cycles. This comprehensive research is the way to tap what the business press refers to as the "hidden" job market. It is paramount that you have as broad a base as possible—people who know people who have a job for you to fill.

With the addition of all those companies to your map, you will have a glittering panorama of prospects, the beginnings of a dossier on each one, and an efficient way of finding any company's exact location. That is useful for finding your way to an interview and in evaluating the job offers coming your way.

Adequate research and preparation is the very foundation for performing well at interviews. And the more interviews you have, the more your research skills will increase; they are the first step to putting yourself in a seller's market.

2.
All Things to
All People

Interviewers today are continually asking for detailed examples of your past performance. They safely assume you will do at least as well (or as poorly) on the new job as you did on the old one, and so the examples you give will seal your fate. Therefore, you need to examine your past performance in a practical manner that will assure you handle these questions correctly.

This chapter will show you how to identify the examples from your past that will impress any interviewer. There is a special bonus: You will also get the correctly packaged information for a workmanlike resume. Two birds with one stone.

Resumes, of course, are important, and there are two facts you must know about them. First, you are going to need one. Second, no one will want to read it. The average interviewer has never been trained to interview effectively, probably finds the interview as uncomfortable as you do, and will do everything possible to avoid discomfort. Resumes, therefore, are used more to screen people out than screen them in. So your resume must be all things to all people.

Another hurdle to clear is avoiding too much of your professional jargon in the resume. It is a cold hard fact that the first person to see your resume is often in the personnel department. This office screens for many different jobs and cannot be expected to have an in-depth knowledge of every specialty within the company—or its special language.

For those reasons, your resume must be short, be easy to read and understand, and use words that are familiar to the reader and that have universal appeal. Most important, it should portray you as a problem-solver.

While this chapter covers ways to build an effective resume, its main goal is to help you perform better at the interview. You will achieve that as you evaluate your professional skills according to the exercises. In fact, you are likely to discover skills and achievements you didn't even know you had. A few you will use in your resume (merely a preview of coming attractions); the others you will use to knock 'em dead at the interview.

A good starting point is your current or last job title. Write it down. Then, jot down all the other different titles you have heard that describe that job. When you are finished, follow it with a three- or four-sentence description of your job functions. Don't think too hard about it, just do it. The titles and descriptions are not carved in stone—this written description is just the beginning of the resume-building exercises. You'll be surprised at what you've written; it will read better than you had thought.

All attributes that you discover and develop in the following exercises are valuable to an employer. You possess many desirable traits, and these exercises help to reveal and to package them.

☐ **Exercise One:** Reread the written job description, then write down your most important duty/function. Follow that with a list of the skills or special training necessary to perform that duty. Next, list the achievements of which you are most proud in that area. It could look something like this:

> Duty: Train and motivate sales staff of six.
>
> Skills: Formal training skills. Knowledge of market and ability to make untrained sales staff productive. Ability to keep successful salespeople motivated and tied to the company.
>
> Achievements: Reduced turnover seven percent; increased sales 14 percent.

The potential employer is most interested in the achievements—those things that make you stand out from the crowd. Try to appeal to a company's interests by conservatively estimating what your achievements meant to your employer. If your achievements saved time, estimate how much. If you saved money, how much? If your achievements made money for the company, how much? Beware of exaggeration—if you were part of a team, identify your achievements as such. It will make your claims more believable and will demonstrate your ability to work with others.

Achievements, of course, differ according to your profession. Most of life's jobs fall into one of these broad categories:

- sales and service;
- management and administration·
- technical and production.

While it is usual to cite the differences between those major job functions, at this point it is far more valuable to you to recognize the commonalities. In sales, dollar volume is important. In management or administration, the parallel is time saved, which is money saved; saving money is just the same as making money for your company. In the technical and production areas, increasing production (doing more in less time) accrues exactly the same benefits to the company. Job titles may differ, yet all employees have the same opportunity to benefit their employers, and in turn, themselves.

The computer revolution of the seventies and the major economic trends of the eighties have irrevocably changed the workplace. Today, companies are doing more with less; they are leaner, have higher expectations of their employees, and plan to keep it that way. The people who get hired and get ahead today are those with a basic understanding of business goals. And successful job candidates are those who have the best interests of the company and its profitability constantly in mind.

□ **Exercise Two:** This simple exercise helps you get a clear picture of your achievements. If you were to meet with your supervisor to discuss a raise, what achievements would you want to discuss? List all you can think of, quickly. Then come back and flesh out the details.

□ **Exercise Three:** This exercise is particularly valuable if you feel you can't see the forest for the trees.

> Problem: Think of a job-related problem you had to face in the last couple of years. Come on, everyone can remember one.

> Solution: Describe your solution to the problem, step by step. List everything you did.

> Results: Finally, consider the results of your solution in terms that would have value to an employer: money earned or saved; time saved.

□ **Exercise Four:** Now, a valuable exercise that turns the absence of a negative into a positive. This one helps you look at your job in a different light and accents important but often overlooked areas that help make you special. Begin discovering for yourself some of the key personal traits that all companies look for.

First, consider actions that if not done properly would affect the goal of your job. If that is difficult, remember an incompetent co-worker. What did he or she do wrong? What did he or she do differently from competent employees?

Now, turn the absence of those negatives into positive attributes. For example, think of the employee who never managed to get to work on time. You could honestly say that someone who did come to work on time every day was punctual and reliable, believed in systems and procedures, was efficiency-minded, and cost- and profit-conscious.

If you have witnessed the reprimands and ultimate termination of that tardy employee, you will see the value of the positive traits in the eyes of an employer. The absence of negative traits makes you a desirable employee, but no one will know unless you say. On completion of the exercise, you will be able to make points about your background in a positive fashion. You will set yourself apart from others, if only because others do not understand the benefit of projecting all their positive attributes.

☐ **Exercise Five:** Potential employers and interviewers are always interested in people who:

- are efficiency-minded;
- have an eye for economy;
- follow procedures;
- are profit-oriented.

Proceed through your work history and identify the aspects of your background that exemplify those traits. These newly discovered personal plusses will not only be woven into your resume, but will be reflected in the posture of your answers when you get to the interview, and in your performance when you land the right job.

Now you need to take some of that knowledge and package it in a resume. There are three standard types of resumes:

Chronological: The most frequently used format. Use it when your work history is stable and your professional growth is consistent. The chronological format is exactly what it sounds like: It follows your work history backwards from the current job, listing companies and dates and responsibilities. Avoid it if you have experienced performance problems, have not grown professionally (but want to), or have made frequent job changes. All those problems will show up in a glaring fashion if you use a chronological resume.

Functional: Use this type if you have been unemployed for long periods of time or have jumped jobs too frequently, or if your career has been stagnant and you want to jump-start it. A functional resume is created without employment dates or company names, and concentrates on skills and responsibilities. It can be useful if you have changed careers, or when current responsibilities don't relate specifically to the job you want. It is written with the most relevant experience to the job you're seeking placed first, and de-emphasizes jobs, employment dates and job titles by placing them inconspicuously at the end. It allows you to promote specific job skills without emphasizing where or when you developed those skills.

Combination: Use this format if you have a steady work history with demonstrated growth, and if you have nothing you wish to de-emphasize. A combination resume is a combination of chronological and functional resumes. It starts with a brief personal summary, then lists job-specific skills relevant to the objective, and segues into a chronological format that lists the how, where, and when these skills were acquired.

Notice that each style is designed to emphasize strengths and minimize certain undesirable traits. In today's world, all of us need a powerful resume. It is not only a door-opener, it is also there long after we are gone and will almost certainly be reviewed just before the choice of the successful candidate is made by the interviewer.

Creating a resume that knocks 'em dead is an art all to itself, and something that is beyond the scope of this book, which concentrates on the conversations that will land interviews and job offers.

If you already have a resume and just want to make sure it measures up, check it against these seven basic rules of resume writing.

☐ **Rule One:** Use the most general of job titles. You are, after all, a hunter of interviews, not of specific titles. Cast your net wide. Use a title that is specific enough to put you in the field, yet vague enough to elicit further questions. One way you can make a job title specifically vague is to add the term "specialist" (e.g., Computer Specialist, Administration Specialist, Production Specialist).

☐ **Rule Two:** Avoid giving a job objective. If you must state a specific job as your goal, couch it in terms of contributions you can make in that position. Do not state what you expect of the employer.

☐ **Rule Three:** Do not state your current salary. If you are earning too little or too much, you could rule yourself out before getting your foot in the door. For the same reason, do not mention your desired salary.

☐ **Rule Four:** Remember that people get great joy from getting pleasant surprises. Show a little gold now, but let the interviewer discover the motherlode at the interview.

☐ **Rule Five:** Try to keep your resume to one page; take whatever steps necessary to keep the resume no more than two pages long. No one reads long resumes—they are boring, and every company is frightened that if it lets in a windbag, it will never get him or her out again.

☐ **Rule Six:** Your resume must be typed. As a rule of thumb, three pages of double-spaced, handwritten notes make one typewritten page.

☐ **Rule Seven:** Finally, emphasize your achievements and problem-solving skills. Keep the resume general.

(For more detailed information on assembling a winning resume, you may wish to purchase this book's companion volume, *Resumes that Knock 'em Dead*—or, if you have a PC, the software based on that book: *The Instant Resume Writer*, from Lightning Word.)

3.
The Executive Briefing

A general resume does have drawbacks. First, it is too general to relate your qualifications to each specific job. Second, more than one person will probably be interviewing you, and that is a major stumbling block. While you will ultimately report to one person, you may well be interviewed by other team members. When that happens, the problems begin.

A manager says, "Spend a few minutes with this candidate and tell me what you think." Your general resume may be impressive, but the manager rarely adequately outlines the job being filled or the specific qualifications for which he or she is looking. This means that other interviewers do not have any way to qualify you fairly and specifically. While the manager will be looking for specific skills relating to projects at hand, personnel will be trying to match your skills to the job-description-manual vagaries, and the other interviewers will fumble in the dark because no one told them what to look for. Such problems can reduce your chances of landing a job offer.

A neat trick I helped develop for the executive-search industry is the Executive Briefing. It enables you to customize your resume quickly to each specific job and acts as a focusing device for whoever interviews you.

Like many great ideas, the Executive Briefing is beautiful in its simplicity. It is a sheet of paper with the company's requirements for the job opening listed on the left side, and your skills—matching point by point the company's needs—on the right. It looks like this:

Executive Briefing

Dear Sir/Madam:

   While my attached resume will provide you with a general outline of my work history, my problem-solving abilities, and some achievements, I have taken the time to list your current specific requirements and my applicable skills in those areas. I hope this will enable you to use your time effectively today.

Your Requirements:	My Skills:
1. Management of public library service area (for circulation, reference, etc.).	1. Experience as head reference librarian at University of Smithtown.
2. Supervision of 14 full-time support employees	2. Supervised support staff of 17.
3. Ability to work with larger supervisory team in planning, budgeting, and policy formulating.	3. During my last year, I was responsible for budget and reformation of circulation rules.
4. ALA-accredited MLS.	4. ALA-accredited MLS.
5. 3 years' experience.	5. 1 year with public library; 2 with University of Smithtown.

   This briefing assures that each resume you send out addresses the job's specific needs and that every interviewer at that company will be interviewing you for the same job.

   Send an Executive Briefing with every resume; it will substantially increase your chances of obtaining an interview with the company. An Executive Briefing sent with a resume provides a comprehensive picture of a thorough professional, plus a personalized, fast, and easy-to-read synopsis that details exactly how you can help with current needs.

   The use of an Executive Briefing is naturally restricted to jobs that you have discovered through your own efforts or seen advertised. It is obviously not appropriate for sending when the requirements of a specific job are unavailable. By following the directions in the next chapter, however, you will be able to use it frequently and effectively. Finally, using the Executive Briefing as a cover letter to your resume will greatly increase the chance that your query will be picked out of the pile in the personnel department and hand carried to the appropriate manager.

II

Getting
to
Square One

With the grunt work completed, you are loaded for bear and ready to knock 'em dead. So how do you begin?

What are your choices? Read the want ads? Everybody else does. Apply for jobs listed with the unemployment office? Everybody else does. Send resumes to companies on the off-chance they have a job that fits your resume? Everybody else does. Or, of course, you can wait for someone to call you. Employ those tactics as your main thrust for hunting down the best jobs in town, and you will fail as do millions of others who fall into the trap of using such outdated job-hunting techniques.

When you look like a penguin, act like a penguin, and hide among penguins, don't be surprised if you get lost in the flock. Today's business marketplace demands a different approach. Your career does not take care of itself—you must go out and grab the opportunities. Grant yourself the right to pick and choose among many job offers with a guaranteed approach: Picking up the telephone.

"Hello, Mr. Smith? My name is Martin Yate. I am an experienced training specialist. . . ."

It's as easy as that.

Guide your destiny by speaking directly to the professionals who make their living in the same way you do. A few minutes spent calling different companies from your research dossier, and you will have an interview. When you get one interview from making a few calls, how many do you think could be arranged with a day's concerted effort?

Because you are in control, it is possible to set your multiple interviews close together. This way your interviewing skills improve from one to the next. And soon, instead of scheduling multiple interviews, you can be weighing multiple job offers.

4.
Paint
the Perfect Picture
on the Phone

Before making that first, nerve-racking telephone call, you must be prepared to achieve one of these three goals, listed here in their priority.

- I will arrange a meeting; or

- I will arrange a time to talk further on the phone; or

- I will ask for a lead on a promising job opening elsewhere.

Always keep those goals in mind. By the time you finish the next four chapters, you'll be able to achieve any one of them quickly and easily.

To make the initial phone call a success, all you need to do is paint a convincing word picture of yourself. To start, remember the old saying: "No one really listens—we are all just waiting for our turn to speak." With that in mind, you shouldn't expect to hold anyone's attention for extended periods of time, so the picture you create needs to be brief yet thorough. Most of all, it should be "specifically vague"—specific enough to arouse interest, to make the company representative prick up his or her ears; vague enough to encourage questions, to make him or her pursue you. The aim is to paint a representation of your skills in broad brush strokes with examples of the money-making, money-saving, or time-saving accomplishments all companies like to hear about.

A presentation made over the telephone must possess four characteristics to be successful. These can best be remembered by an old acronym from the advertising world, AIDA:

A–You must get the company representative's *attention*.

I–You must get his or her *interest*.

D–You must create a *desire* in him or her to know more about you.

A–You must encourage him or her to take *action*.

With AIDA you get noticed. The interest you generate will be measured by the questions asked: "How much are you making?" or, "Do you have a degree?" or, "How many years' experience do you have?" By giving the appropriate answers to those and other questions (which I will discuss in detail), you will change interest into a desire to know more and parlay that desire into an interview.

The types of questions you are asked also enable you to identify the company's specific needs. Once they are identified, you can gear the ongoing conversation toward them.

Here are the steps in building your AIDA presentation:

☐ **Step One:** This covers who you are and what you do. It is planned to get the company representative's attention, to give the person a reason to stay on the phone. The introduction will include your job title and a brief generalized description of your duties and responsibilities. Use a non-specific job title, as you did for your resume. Remember: getting a foot in the door with a generalized title can provide the occasion to sell your superior skills.

Tell just enough about yourself to whet the company's appetite, and cause the representative to start asking questions. Again, keep your description a little vague. For example, if you describe yourself as simply "experienced," the company representative must try to qualify your statement with a question: "How much experience do you have?" That way, you establish a level of interest. But, if you describe yourself as having four years' experience, and the company is looking for seven, you are likely to be ruled out without even knowing there was a job to be filled. Never specify exact experience or list all your accomplishments during the initial presentation. Your aim is just to open a dialogue.

Example:

"Good morning, Mr. Smith. My name is Jenny Jones. I am an experienced office-equipment salesperson with an in-depth knowledge of the office-products industry. Have I caught you at a good time?"

Note: Never ask if you have caught someone at a bad time. You are offering them an excuse to say "yes." By the same token, asking whether you have caught someone at a good time will usually get you a "yes." Then you can go directly into the rest of your presentation.

☐ **Step Two:** Now you are ready to generate interest, and from that, desire—it's time to sell one or two of your accomplishments. You already should have identified them during the resume-building exercises. Pull out no more than two items and follow your introductory sentence with them. Keep them brief and to the point, without embellishments.

Example:

"As the #3 salesperson in my company, I increased sales in my territory 15 percent to over $1 million. In the last six months, I won three major accounts from my competitors."

☐ **Step Three:** You have made the company representative want to know more about you, so now you can make him or her take action. Include the reason for your call and a request to meet. It should be carefully constructed to finish with a question that will bring a positive response, which will launch the two of you into a nuts-and-bolts discussion between two professionals.

Example:

"The reason I'm calling, Mr. Smith, is that I'm looking for a new challenge, and having researched your company, I felt we might have some areas for discussion. Are these the types of skills and accomplishments you look for in your staff?"

Your presentation ends with a question that guarantees a positive response, and the conversation gets moving.

Your task now is to write out a presentation applying those guidelines to your work experience. Knowing exactly what you are going to say and what you wish to achieve is the only way to generate multiple interviews and multiple job offers. When your presentation is prepared and written, read it aloud to yourself, and imagine the faceless company representative on the other end of the line. Practice with a friend or spouse, or use a tape recorder to critique yourself.

After you make the actual presentation on the phone, you'll really begin to work on arranging a meeting, scheduling another phone conversation, or establishing a referral. There will likely be a silence on the other end after your initial pitch. Be patient—the company representative needs time to digest your words. If you are tempted to break the silence, resist—you don't want to break the person's train of thought, nor do you want the ball back in your court.

This contemplative silence may last as long as 20 seconds, but when the company representative responds, only three things can happen:

1. The company representative can agree with you and arrange a meeting.

2. He or she can ask questions that show interest.

   Examples:

   • "Do you have a degree?"

   • "How much are you earning?"

Any question, because it denotes interest, is known as a buy signal. And handled properly, it will enable you to arrange a meeting.

3. He or she can raise an objection.

Examples:

- "I don't need anyone like that now."
- "Send me a resume."

Those objections, when handled properly, will also result in an interview with the company, or at least a referral to someone else who has job openings. In fact, you will frequently find that objections prove themselves to be terrific opportunities disguised as unsolvable problems.

I hope you can handle the first option—"Yes, I'd like to meet you"—with little assistance. For obvious reasons, it doesn't get a chapter. Now let's focus on buy signals and objections, and how you can turn them into interviews.

5.
Responding to Buy Signals

With just a touch of nervous excitement you finish your presentation: "Are these the types of skills and accomplishments you look for in your staff?" There is silence on the other end. It is broken by a question. You breathe a sigh of relief because you remember that any question denotes interest and is a buy signal.

Now, conversation is a two-way street, and you are most likely to win an interview when you take responsibility for your half. Just as the employer's questions show interest in you, your questions should show your interest in the work done at the company. By asking questions of your own in the normal course of conversation—questions usually tagged on to the end of one of your answers—you will forward the conversation. Also, such questions help you find out what particular skills and qualities are important to the employer. Inquisitiveness will increase your knowledge of the opportunity at hand, and that knowledge will give you the power to arrange a meeting.

The alternative is to leave all the interrogation to the employer. That will place you on the defensive and at the end of the talk, you will be as ignorant of the real parameters of the job as you were at the start. And the employer will know less about you than you might want.

Applying the technique of giving a short answer and finishing that reply with a question will carry your call to its logical conclusion: The interviewer will tell you the job specifics, and as that happens, you will present the relevant skills or attributes. In any conversation, the person who asks the questions controls its outcome. You called the employer to get an interview as the first step in generating a job offer, so take control of your destiny by taking control of the conversation.

Example:

Jenny Jones: "Good morning, Mr. Smith. My name is Jenny Jones. I am an experienced office-equipment salesperson with an in-depth knowledge of the office-products industry. Have I caught you at a good time? . . . As the #3 salesperson in my company, I increased sales in my territory 15 percent to over $1 million. In the last six months, I won three major accounts from my competitors. The reason I'm calling, Mr. Smith, is that I'm looking for a new challenge, and having researched your company, I felt we might have areas for discussion. Are these the types of skills and accomplishments you look for in your staff?"

[Pause.]

Mr. Smith: "Yes, they are. What type of equipment have you been selling?" *[Buy signal!]*

J: "My company carries a comprehensive range, and I sell both the top and bottom of the line, according to my customers' needs. I have been noticing a considerable interest in the latest fax and scanning equipment." *[You've made it a conversation; you further it with the following.]* "Has that been your experience recently?"

S: "Yes, especially in the color and acetate capability machines." *[Useful information for you.]* "Do you have a degree?" *[Buy signal!]*

J: "Yes, I do." *[Just enough information to keep the company representative chasing you.]* "I understand your company prefers degreed salespeople to deal with its more sophisticated clients." *[Your research is paying off.]*

S: "Our customer base is very sophisticated, and they expect a certain professionalism and competence from us." *[An inkling of the kind of person they want to hire.]* "How much experience do you have?" *[Buy signal!]*

J: "Well, I've worked in both operations and sales, so I have a wide experience base." *[General but thorough.]* "How many years of experience are you looking for?" *[Turning it around, but furthering the conversation.]*

S: "Ideally, four or five for the position I have in mind." *[More good information.]* "How many do you have?" *[Buy signal!]*

J: "I have two with this company, and one and a half before that. I fit right in with your needs, don't you agree?" *[How can Mr. Smith say no?]*

S: "Uhmmm . . . what's your territory?" *[Buy signal!]*

J: "I cover the metropolitan area. Mr. Smith, it really does sound as if we might have something to talk about." *[Remember, your first goal is the face-to-face interview.]* "I am planning to take Thursday and Friday off at the end of the week. Can we meet then?" *[Make Mr. Smith decide what day he can see you, rather than whether he will see you at all.]* "Which would be best for you?"

S: "How about Friday morning? Can you bring a resume?"

Your conversation should proceed with that kind of give-and-take. Your questions show interest, carry the conversation forward, and teach you more about the company's needs. By the end of the conversation you have an interview arranged and several key areas to promote when you arrive:

- company sees growth in the latest fax and scanning equipment, especially those with color and acetate capabilities;

- they want business and personal sophistication;

- they ideally want four or five years' experience;

- they are interested in your metropolitan contacts.

The above is a fairly simple scenario, and even though it is constructive, it doesn't show you the tricky buy signals that can spell disaster in your job hunt. These are questions that appear to be simple buy signals, yet in reality they are a part of every interviewer's arsenal called "knock-out" questions—questions that can save the interviewer time by quickly ruling out certain types of candidates. Although these questions most frequently arise during the initial telephone conversation, they can crop up at the face-to-face interview; the answering techniques are applicable throughout the interview cycle.

Note: We all come from different backgrounds and geographical areas. So understand that while my answers cover correct approaches and responses, they do not attempt to capture the regional and personal flavor of conversation. You and I will never talk alike, so don't learn the example answers parrot-fashion. Instead, you should take the essence of the responses and personalize them until the words fall easily from your lips.

Buy Signal:
"How much are you making/do you want?"
This is a direct question looking for a direct answer, yet it is a knock-out question. Earning either too little or too much could ruin your chances before you're given the opportunity to shine in person. There are a number of options that could serve you better than a direct answer. First, you must understand that questions about money at this point in the conversation are being used to screen you in or screen you out of the ballpark—the answers you give now should be geared specifically toward getting you in the door and into a face-to-face meeting. (Handling the serious salary negotiations that are attached to a job offer is covered extensively in Chapter 21, "Negotiating the Offer," on page 175). For now, your main options are as follows.

□ **Put yourself above the money:** "I'm looking for a job and a company to call home. If I am the right person for you, I'm sure you'll make me a fair offer. What is the salary range for the position?"

☐ **Give a vague answer:** "The most important things to me are the job itself and the company. What is the salary range for the position?"

☐ **Or you could answer a question with a question:** "How much does the job pay?"

When you are pressed a second time for an exact dollar figure, be as honest and forthright as circumstances permit. Some people (often, unfortunately, women) are underpaid for their jobs when their work is compared to that of others in similar positions. It is not a question of perception; these women in fact make less money than they should. If you have the skills for the job and you are concerned that your current low salary will eliminate you before you have the chance to show your worth, you might want to add into your base salary the dollar-value of your benefits. If it turns out to be too much, you can then simply explain that you were including the value of your benefits. Or, you could say, "Mr. Smith, my previous employers felt I am well worth the money I earn due to my skills, dedication, and honesty. Were we to meet, I'm sure I could demonstrate my value and my ability to contribute to your department. You'd like an opportunity to make that evaluation, wouldn't you?"

Notice the "wouldn't you?" at the end of the reply. A reflexive question such as this is a great conversation-forwarding technique because it encourages a positive response. Conservative use of reflexive questions can really help you move things along. Watch the sound of your voice, though. A reflexive question can sound pleasantly conversational or pointed and accusatory; it's not really what you say, but how you say it.

Such questions are easy to create. Just conclude with "wouldn't you?" "didn't you?" "won't you?" "couldn't you?" "shouldn't you?" or "don't you?" as appropriate at the end of virtually any statement, and the interviewer will almost always answer "yes." You have kept the conversation alive, and moved it closer to your goal. Repeat the reflexive questions to yourself. They have a certain rhythm that will help you remember them.

Buy Signal:
"Do you have a degree?"

Always answer the exact question; beware of giving unrequested (and possibly excessive) information. For example, if you have a bachelor's degree in fine arts from New York University, your answer is "Yes," not "Yes, I have a bachelor's degree in fine arts from NYU." Perhaps the company wants an architecture degree. Perhaps the company representative has bad feelings about NYU graduates. You don't want to be knocked out before you've been given the chance to prove yourself.

"Yes, I have a degree. What background are you looking for?" Or, you can always answer a question with a question: "I have a diverse educational background. Ideally, what are you looking for?"

When a degree is perceived as mandatory and you barely scraped through grade school, don't be intimidated. As Calvin Coolidge used to say, "The world is full of educated layabouts." You may want to use the "Life University" answer. For instance: "My education was cut short by the necessity of earning a living at an early age. My past managers have found that my life experience and responsible attitude is a valuable asset to the department. Also, I intend to return to school to continue my education."

A small proportion of the more sensitive employers are verifying educational credentials, and if yours are checked it means the employer takes such matters seriously, so an untruth or an exaggeration could cost you a job. Think hard and long before inflating your educational background.

Buy Signal:
"How much experience do you have?"

Too much or too little could easily rule you out. Be careful how you answer and try to gain time. It is a vague question, and you have a right to ask for qualifications.

"Could you help me with that question?" or, "Are you looking for overall experience or in some specific areas?" or, "Which areas are most important to you?" Again, you answer a question with a question. The employer's response, while gaining you time, tells you what it takes to do the job and therefore what you have to say to get it, so take mental notes—you can even write them down, if you have time. Then give an appropriate response.

You might want to retain control of the conversation by asking another question, for example: "The areas of expertise you require sound very interesting, and it sounds as if you have some exciting projects at hand. Exactly what projects would I be involved with in the first few months?"

After one or two buy signal questions are asked, ask for a meeting. Apart from those just outlined, questions asked over the phone tend not to contain traps. If you simply ask, "Would you like to meet me?" there are only two possible responses: yes or no. Your chances of success are greatly decreased. When you intimate, however, that you will be in the area on a particular date or dates—"I'm going to be in town on Thursday and Friday, Mr. Smith. Which would be better for you?"—you have asked a question that moves the conversation along dramatically. Your question gives the company representative the choice of meeting you on Thursday or Friday, rather than meeting you or not meeting you. By presuming the "yes," you reduce the chances of hearing a negative, and increase the possibility of a face-to-face meeting.

6.
Responding to Objections

Even with the most convincing word picture, the silence may be broken not by a buy signal, but by an objection. An objection is usually a statement, not a question: "Send me a resume," or, "I don't have time to see you," or, "You are earning too much," or, "You'll have to talk to personnel," or, "I don't need anyone like you right now."

Although these seem like brush-off lines, often they are really disguised opportunities to get yourself a job offer—handled properly, almost all objections can be parlayed into interviews. This section will teach you to seize hidden opportunities successfully; notice that all your responses have a commonality with buy-signal responses. They all end with a question, one that will enable you to learn more about the reason for the objection, overcome it, and once again lead the conversation toward a face-to-face interview.

In dealing with objections, as with differences of opinion, nothing is gained by confrontation, though much is to be gained by appreciation of the other's viewpoint. Most objections you hear are best handled by first demonstrating your understanding of the other's viewpoint. Always start your response with "I understand," or, "I can appreciate your position," or, "I see your point," or, "Of course," followed by, "However," or, "Also consider," or a similar line that puts you back into consideration.

Remember, these responses should not be learned merely to be repeated. You need only to understand and implement their meaning, to understand their concept and put the answers in your own words. Personalize all the suggestions to your character and style of speech.

Objection:

"Why don't you send me a resume?"

Danger here. The company representative may be genuinely interested in seeing your resume as a first step in the interview cycle; or it may be a polite way of getting you off the phone. You should identify what the real reason is without causing antagonism. At the same time, you want to open up the conversation. A good reply would be: "Of course, Mr. Smith. Would you give me your exact title and the full address? . . . Thank you. So that I can be sure that my qualifications fit your needs, what skills are you looking for in this position?"

Notice the steps:

- apparent agreement to start;

- a show of consideration;

- a question to further the conversation.

Answering in that fashion will open up the conversation. Mr. Smith will relay the aspects of the job that are important to him, and with this knowledge, you can sell Smith on your skills over the phone. Also, you will be able to use the information to draw attention to your skills in the future, in:

- following conversations;

- the cover letter to your resume;

- your executive briefing;

- your face-to-face meeting;

- your follow-up after the meeting.

The information you glean will give you power and will increase your chances of receiving a job offer.

□ □ □

Objection:

"I don't have time to see you."

If the employer is too busy to see you, he or she has a problem, and by recognizing that, perhaps you can show yourself as the one to solve it. You should avoid confrontation, however—it is important that you demonstrate empathy for the speaker. Agree, empathize, and ask a question that moves the conversation forward.

"I understand how busy you must be; it sounds like a competent, dedicated, and efficient professional [whatever your title is] could be of some assistance. Perhaps I could call you back at a better time, to discuss how I might make you some time. When are you least busy, the morning or afternoon?"

The company representative will either make time to talk now, or will arrange a better time for the two of you to talk further.

Here are some other ideas you could use to phrase the same objection:

"Since you are so busy, what is the best time of day for you? First thing in the morning, or is the afternoon a quieter time?" or, "I will be in your area tomorrow, so why don't I come by and see you?"

Of course, you can combine the two: "I'm going to be in your part of town tomorrow, and I could drop by and see you. What is your quietest time, morning or afternoon?" By presuming the invitation for a meeting, you make it harder for the company representative to object. And if he or she is truly busy, your consideration will be appreciated and still make it hard to object.

Objection:
"You are earning too much."

You should not have brought up salary in the first place. Go straight to jail. If the company representative brought up the matter, that's a buy signal, which was discussed in the last chapter. If the job really doesn't pay enough, you got (as the carnival barker says) close, but no cigar! How to make a success of this seeming deadend is handled in the next chapter. You may also refer to helpful information covered in Chapter 19, "Negotiating the Offer."

Objection:
"We only promote from within."

Your response could be: "I realize that, Mr. Smith. Your development of employees is a major reason I want to get in! I am bright, conscientious, and motivated. When you do hire from the outside, what assets are you looking for?"

The response finishes with a question designed to carry the conversation forward, and to give you a new opportunity to sell yourself. Notice that the response assumes that the company is hiring from the outside, even though the company representative has said otherwise. You have called his bluff, but in a professional, inoffensive manner.

Objection:
"You'll have to talk to personnel."

Your reply is: "Of course, Mr. Smith. Whom should I speak to in personnel, and what specific position should I mention?"

You cover a good deal of ground with that response. You establish whether there is a job there or whether you are being fobbed off to personnel to waste their time and your own. Also, you move the conversation forward again, and have changed the thrust of it to your advantage. Develop a specific job-related question to ask while the company representative is answering the first question. It can open a fruitful line for you to pursue. If you receive a non-specific reply, probe a little deeper. A simple phrase like, "That's interesting, please tell me more," or, "Why's that?" will usually do the trick.

Or you can ask: "When I speak to personnel, will it be about a specific job you have, or is it to see whether I might fill a position elsewhere in the company?"

Armed with the resulting information, you can talk to personnel about your conversation with Mr. Smith. Remember to get the name of a specific person with whom to speak, and to quote the company representative.

Example:
"Good morning, Mr. Johnson. Mr. Smith, the regional sales manager, suggested we should speak to arrange an interview."

That way, you will show personnel that you are not a waste of time; because you know someone in the company, you won't be regarded as one of the frequent "blind" calls they get every day. As the most overworked, understaffed department in a company, they will appreciate that. Most important, you will stand out, be noticed.

Don't look at the personnel department as a roadblock; it may contain a host of opportunities for you. Because a large company may have many different departments that can use your talents, personnel is likely to be the only department that knows all the openings. You might be able to arrange three or four interviews with the same company for three or four different positions!

Objection:
"I really wanted someone with a degree."
You could respond to this by saying: "Mr. Smith, I appreciate your position. It was necessary that I start earning a living early in life. If we meet, I am certain you would recognize the value of my additional practical experience."

You might then wish to ask what the company policy is for support and encouragement of employees taking night classes or continuing-education courses, and will naturally explain how you are hoping to find an employer who encourages employees to further their education. Your response will end with: "If we were to meet, I am certain you would recognize the value of my practical experience. I am going to be in your area next week. When would be the best time of day to get together?"

Objection:

"I don't need anyone like you now."

Short of suggesting that the employer fire someone to make room for you (which, incidentally, has been done successfully on a few occasions), chances of getting an interview with this particular company are slim. With the right question, however, that person will give you a personal introduction to someone else who could use your talents. Asking that right question or series of questions is what networking and the next chapter are all about. So on the occasions when the techniques for answering buy signals or rebutting objections do not get you a meeting, "Getting Live Leads From Dead Ends" will!

7.
Getting Live Leads From Dead Ends

There will be times when you have said all the right things on the phone, but hear, "I can't use anyone like you right now." Not every company has a job opening for you, nor are you right for every job. Sometimes you must accept a temporary setback and understand that the rejection is not one of you as a human being. By using these special interview development questions, though, you will be able to turn those setbacks into job interviews.

The company representative is a professional and knows other professionals in his or her field, in other departments, subsidiaries, even other companies. If you approach the phone presentation in a professional manner, he or she, as a fellow professional, will be glad to advise you on who is looking for someone with your skills. Nearly everyone you call will be pleased to head you in the right direction, but only if you *ask!* And you'll be able to ask as many questions as you wish, because you will be recognized as a colleague intelligently using the professional network. The company representative also knows that his good turn in referring you to a colleague at another company will be returned in the future. And, as a general rule, companies prefer candidates to be referred this way over any other method.

But do not expect people to be clairvoyant. There are two sayings: "You get what you ask for," and "If you don't ask, you don't get." Each is pertinent here.

When you are sure that no job openings exist within a particular department, ask one of these questions:

- "Who else in the company might need someone with my qualifications?"

- "Does your company have any other divisions or subsidiaries that might need someone with my attributes?"

- "Whom do you know in the business community who might have a lead for me?"

- "Which are the most rapidly growing companies in the area?"

- "Whom should I speak to there?"

- "Do you know anyone at the ABC Electronics Company?"

- "When do you anticipate an opening in your company?"

- "Are you planning any expansion or new projects that might create an opening?"

- "When do you anticipate change in your manpower needs?"

Each one of those interview-development questions can gain you an introduction or lead to a fresh opportunity. The questions have not been put in any order of importance—that is for you to do. Take a sheet of paper and, looking at the list, figure out what question you would ask if you had time to ask only one. Write it down. Do that with the remaining questions on the list. As you advance, you will develop a comfortable set of prioritized questions. Add questions of your own. For instance, the type of computer or word-processing equipment a company has might be important to some professions, but not to others, and a company representative might be able to lead you to companies that have your machines. Be sure that any question you add to your list is specific and leads to a job opening. Avoid questions like, "How's business these days?" Time is valuable, and time is money to both of you. When you're satisfied with your list of interview development questions, put them on a fresh sheet of paper and store it safely with your telephone presentation and resume.

Those interview development questions will lead you to a substantial number of jobs in the hidden job market. You are getting referrals from the "in" crowd, who know who is hiring whom long before that news is generally circulated. By being in with the "in" crowd, you establish a very effective referral network.

When you get leads on companies and specific individuals to talk to, be sure to thank your benefactor and ask to use his or her name as an introduction. The answer, you will find, will always be "yes," but asking shows you to be someone with manners—in this day and age, that alone will set you apart.

You might also suggest to your contact that you leave your telephone number in case he or she runs into someone who can use you. You'll be surprised at how many people call back with a lead.

With personal permission to use someone's name on your next networking call, you have been given the greatest of job-search gifts: a personal introduction. Your call will begin with something like:

"Hello, Ms. Smith. My name is Jack Jones. Joseph McDonald recommended I give you a call. By the way, he sends his regards." [Pause for any response to this.] "He felt we might have something valuable to discuss."

Follow up on every lead you get. Too many people become elated at securing an interview for themselves and then cease all effort to generate additional interviews, believing a job offer is definitely on its way. Your goal is to have a choice of the best jobs in town, and without multiple interviews, there is no way you'll have that choice. Asking interview-development questions ensures that you are tapping all the secret recesses of the hidden job market.

Networking is a continuous cycle:

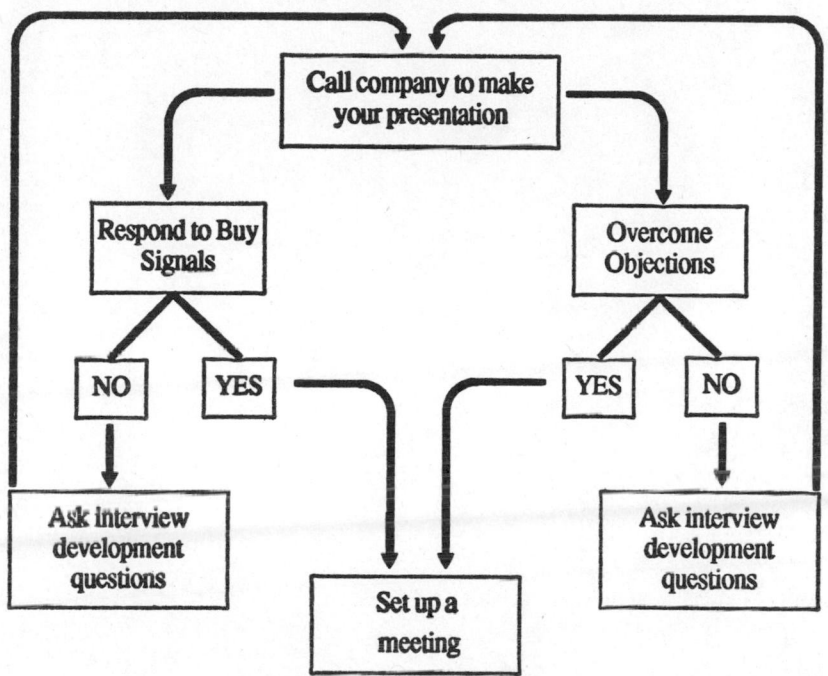

Make a commitment to sell yourself, to make telephone calls, to make a referral network, to recognize buy signals and objections for what they really are—opportunities to shine. Make a commitment to ask interview-development questions at every seeming dead end: They will lead you to all the jobs in town.

8.
The Telephone Interview

In this glorious technological age, the first substantive contact with a potential employer is virtually always by telephone. It's the way business is done today. It happens in one of three ways:

- when you are networking, and the company representative goes into a screening process immediately because you have aroused his or her interest;

- a company calls unexpectedly as a result of a resume you have mailed, and catches you off-guard;

- you or a headhunter who has agreed to take you on has set up a specific time for a telephone interview.

Whatever circumstance creates the telephone interview, you must be prepared to handle the questioning and use every means at your disposal to win the real thing—the face-to-face meeting. The telephone interview is the trial run for the face-to-face and is an opportunity you must not bumble; your happiness and prosperity may hinge on it.

This, the first contact with your future employer, will test your mental preparation. Remember: You can plant in your mind any thought, plan, desire, strategy, or purpose, and translate it into reality. Put your goal down on paper and read it aloud to yourself every day, because the constant reiteration will crystallize your aims, and clear goals provide the most solid base of preparation.

Being prepared for a telephone interview takes organization. You never know when a company is going to call once you have started networking and sending your resume out (the word gets around more quickly than you think if it's a resume that knocks 'em dead). Usually the call comes at the worst of times, such as 8 o'clock Monday morning when you are sleeping late, or 4:56 in the afternoon, just as you return from walking the dog. You can avoid being caught completely off-guard by keeping your resume and alphabetized company dossiers by the telephone.

The most obvious (and often most neglected) point to remember is this: During the interview, the company representative has only ears with which to judge you, and that is something you must overcome. Here are some tips.

- **Take a surprise call in stride.** If you receive a call as a result of a mailed resume or a telephone message you left, and you are unprepared, be calm. Sound positive, friendly, and collected: "Thank you for calling, Mr. Smith. Would you wait just a moment while I close the door?"

  Put the phone down, take three deep breaths to slow your heart down, pull out the appropriate company dossier and your resume, put a smile on your face (it improves the timbre of your voice), and pick up the phone again. Now you are in control of yourself and the situation.

- **Beware of over-familiarity.** You should always refer to the interviewer by his or her surname until invited to do otherwise.

- **Allow the company representative to do most of the talking**—to ask most (but not all) of the questions. Keep up your end of the conversation—this is, after all, a sales presentation, so be sure to ask a few questions of your own that will reveal you as an intelligent person and provide you the opportunity to promote your candidacy. For example, ask what immediate projects the interviewer's department is involved in, or the biggest challenges that are being tackled. When the interviewer answers your question, you will either have a clear picture of how to sell yourself, or you will ask a follow-up question for clarification.

  For example: "What specific skills and personality traits do you think are necessary for a person to succeed with those challenges?" Everyone hires a problem-solver—find the problem and you are already halfway toward the offer.

- **Beware of giving yes/no answers.** They give no real information about your abilities.

- **Be factual in your answers.** Brief yet thorough.

- **Speak directly into the telephone.** Keep the mouthpiece about one inch from your mouth. Do not smoke or eat while on the phone. Numbered among the mystical properties of our telephone system is its excellence at picking up and amplifying background music and voices, especially young ones. That is excelled only by its power to transmit the sounds of food or gum being chewed or smoke being inhaled or exhaled. Smokers, take note: there are no laws about discriminating against smokers, and therefore, all non-smokers naturally discriminate. They will assume that even if you don't actually light up at the interview, you'll have been chain-smoking beforehand and will carry the smell with you as long as you are around. Taking no chances, they probably won't even give you a chance to get through the door once they hear you puffing away over the phone.

- **Take notes.** They will be invaluable to you in preparing for the face-to-face meeting. Were it not for the recent furor over the clandestine use of tape recorders, I would have recommended that you buy a cheap tape recorder and a phone attachment from your local electronics store and tape the whole conversation.

  If, for any reason, the company representative is interrupted, jot down the topic under discussion. When he or she gets back on the line, you can helpfully recap: "We were just discussing . . ." That will be appreciated and will set you apart from the others.

The company representative may talk about the corporation, and from the dossier in front of you, you will also know facts about the outfit. A little flattery goes a long way: Admire the company's achievements and you are, in fact, admiring the interviewer. Likewise, if any areas of common interest arise, comment on them, and agree with the interviewer when possible—people hire people like themselves.

If the interviewer does not give you the openings you need to sell yourself, be ready to salvage the situation and turn it to your advantage. Have a few work-related questions prepared—for example, "What exactly will be the three major responsibilities in this job?" or, "What will be the first job I get my teeth into?" While you are getting the explanation, wait for a pause so that you can tell the interviewer your appropriate skills: "Would it be of value if I described my experience in the area of office management?" or, "Then my experience in word processing should be a great help to you," or, "I recently completed an accounting project just like that."

Under no circumstances, though, should you ask about the money you want, or benefits and vacation time; that comes later.

Remember that your single objective at this point is to sell yourself and your skills; if you don't do that, you may never get the face-to-face interview.

The telephone interview has come to an end when you are asked whether you have any questions. Ask any more questions that will improve your understanding of the job requirements. If you haven't asked before, now is the time to establish what projects you would be working on in the first six months. By discovering them now, you will have time before the face-to-face meeting to package your skills to the needs at hand, and to create the appropriate Executive Briefing.

And if you have not already asked or been invited to meet the interviewer, now is the time. Take the initiative.

"It sounds like a very interesting opportunity, Ms. Smith, and a situation where I could definitely make a contribution. The most pressing question I have now is, when can we get together?" [*Note:* Even though the emphasis throughout has been on putting things in your own words, do use "make a contribution." It shows pride in your work—a key personal trait.]

Once the details are confirmed, finish with this request: "If I need any additional information before the interview, I would like to feel free to get back to you." The company representative will naturally agree. No matter how many questions you get answered in the initial conversation, there will always be something you forget. This allows you to call again to satisfy any curiosity—it will also enable you to increase rapport. Don't take too much advantage of it, though: One well-placed phone call that contains two or three considered questions will be appreciated; four or five phone calls will not.

Taking care to ascertain the correct spelling and pronunciation of the interviewer's name shows your concern for the small but important things in life—it will be noticed. This is also a good time to establish who else will be interviewing you, their titles, and how long the meeting is expected to last.

Follow with a casual inquiry as to what direction the meeting will take. You might ask, "Would you tell me some of the critical areas we will discuss on Thursday?" The knowledge gained will help you to package and present yourself, and will allow you time to bone up on any weak or rusty areas.

It is difficult to evaluate an opportunity properly over the telephone. Even if the job doesn't sound right, go to the interview. It will give you practice, and the job may look better when you have more facts. You might even discover a more suitable opening elsewhere within the company when you go to the face-to-face interview.

9.
Dressing for Interview Success

The moment we set eyes on someone, our minds make evaluations and judgments with lightning speed. The same is true for the potential employers who must assess us.

"What you see is what you get!"

"If a candidate can't put himself together in a professional manner, why should you assume he can put it all together on the job? Unless you look the part, don't expect an offer!" It may sound harsh, but that's an accurate summary of most employers' feelings on this issue. It's a fair estimate that nine out of ten of today's employers will reject an unsuitably dressed applicant without a second thought. Similarly dispiriting odds confront those who expect promotions but wear less than appropriate attire on the job. Like it or not, your outward image, your attitude, your confidence level, and your overall delivery are all affected by the clothes you wear.

The respect you receive at the interview is in direct proportion to the respect your visual image earns for you before you have the chance to say a word. If you wear clothes that are generally associated with leisure activities, you may be telling those who see you that you do not take your career seriously, and therefore are not committed to your work. Similarly, if you report for work the first day on a new job wearing clothes that undercut your perceived effectiveness, personal skills, and professionalism, it will be hard for you to be seen as a major contributor—no matter what you do between nine and five.

Employers rarely make overt statements about acceptable dress codes to their employees, much less to interviewees; more often, there is an unspoken dictum that those who wish to climb the professional career ladder will dress appropriately . . . and that those who don't, won't.

There are some areas of employment where on-the-job dress (as opposed to interview dress) is somewhat less conservative than in the mainstream: fashion, entertainment, and advertising are three examples. In these and a few other fields, there is a good deal of leeway with regard to personal expression in workplace attire. But for most of us, our jobs and our employers require a certain minimal level of professionalism in our dress. Interviewees must exceed these standards. This is not to say that you must dress like the chairman of the board (although that probably won't hurt), but you should be aware that dressing for the Friday night Lambada party on the day of your interview is not in your best professional interests.

Dressing Sharp: Your Interviewing Advantage

Our appearance tells people how we feel about ourselves as applicants, as well as how we feel about the interviewer(s), the company, and the process of interviewing itself. By dressing professionally, we tell people that we understand the niceties of corporate life, and we send a subtle "reinforcing" message that we can, for example, be relied upon to deal one-on-one with members of a company's prized client base.

More to the point, the correct image at an interview will give you a real edge over your competition. In fact, your overall appearance and presentation may well leave a more tangible impression than the words you say, since memory is rooted most strongly in pictures and impressions. At the very least, you can expect what you say to be strongly influenced in the mind of your interviewer by the way you present yourself.

Of course, the act of taking time to present an attractive professional image before you interview will add to your own sense of self-esteem and confidence. That is perhaps the greatest advantage of all.

The Look

The safest look for both men and women at interviews is traditional and conservative. This makes life fairly easy for the men: their professional fashions tend not to change much from year to year. A man can usually interview with confidence and poise in his three-year-old Brooks Brothers suit, provided that it isn't worn to a shine.

For women, the matter is a little more complicated. Appropriate female attire for the interview should ideally reflect the current fashion if the applicant is to be taken seriously. Rarely, if ever, can a woman feel comfortable interviewing in something she bought several years ago. Moreover, in selecting her current professional "uniform" the female applicant must walk a thin line, combining elements of both conformity (to show she belongs) and panache (to show a measure of individuality and style).

The key for both sexes is to dress for the position you want, not the one you have. This means that the upwardly mobile professional might need to invest in the clothes that project the desired image. The woman who dresses like a long-term member of the steno pool is unlikely ever to leave the secretarial ranks; the man who dresses like one of the corporate walking wounded will never be invited to move to Mahogany Row. Positions of responsibility are awarded to those who demonstrate that they are able to shoulder the burden. *Looking* capable will inspire others with the confidence to give you the most visible challenges.

The correct appearance alone probably won't get you a job offer, but it will go a long way toward winning attention and respect. When you know you look right, you can stop worrying about the impression your clothes are making and concentrate on communicating your message.

To be sure, every interview and every interviewer is different; because of this, it isn't possible to set down rigid guidelines for exactly what to wear in each situation. There is, however, relevant broadly based counsel that will help you make the right decision for your interview.

As we have seen, much of what we believe about others is based on our perception of their appearance; this chapter will help you insure that you are perceived as practical, well educated, competent, ethical, and professional.

General Guidelines

Appropriate attire, as we have noted, varies from industry to industry. The college professor can sport tweed jackets with elbow patches on the job, but is nevertheless likely to wear a suit to an interview. The advertising executive may wear wild ties as a badge of creativity (that is what he is being paid for), but he too is likely to dress conservatively for an interview. In all instances, our clothes are sending a message about our image, and the image we want to convey is one of reliability, trustworthiness, and attention to detail.

Most of us are far more adept at recognizing the dress mistakes of others than at spotting our own sartorial failings. When we do look for a second opinion, we often make the mistake of only asking a loved one. It's not that spouses, lovers, and parents lack taste; these people are, however, more in tune with our positive qualities than the rest of the world, and frequently they do not recognize how essential it is to reflect those qualities in our dress. Better candidates for evaluation of your interview attire are trusted friends who have proved their objectivity in such matters, or even a colleague at work.

Whenever possible, find out the dress code of the company you are visiting. For example, if you are an engineer applying for a job at a high-tech company, a blue three-piece suit might be overpowering. It is perfectly acceptable to ask someone in personnel about the dress code (written or informal) of the company. In the example we just used, you might be perfectly comfortable showing up *for work* in a sports coat or blazer; nevertheless, you are advised to wear a suit, at least for the first interview.

You may simply decide to change your look somewhat after learning of a more informal atmosphere with regard to dress at the firm you visit. If you are told that everyone works in shirt-sleeves and that there is never a tie in sight, a prudent and completely acceptable approach is to opt for your less formal brown or beige suit, rather than blues, grays, or pinstripes.

Men

Following are the best current dress guidelines for men preparing for a professional interview.

Men's Suits

The most acceptable colors for men's suits are navy through teal blue and charcoal through light gray, followed at some distance by brown and beige. The fabric should be 100% wool; wool looks and wears better than any other material. Stay away from European designer suits, as they tend to be cut tighter and are often too flashy for the conservative world we live in. Two-piece suits are completely acceptable today, whereas only a few years ago one had to wear a three-piece suit to an interview.

The darker the suit, the more authority it carries (but beware: a man should *not* wear a black suit to an interview unless applying for an undertaker's job). Solid colors and pinstripes are both acceptable, so long as the stripes themselves are muted and very narrow. Of the solids, dark gray, navy, or teal blue are equally acceptable. Some feel that a dark solid suit is the best option, because it gives authority to the wearer and is less intimidating than a pinstripe suit.

Men's Shirts

The principles here are simple.

Rule One: Always wear a long-sleeved shirt.

Rule Two: Always wear a white or pale blue shirt.

Rule Three: Never violate Rules One or Two.

By "white," I do not mean to exclude, for instance, shirts with very thin red or blue pinstripes: these "white" shirts are acceptable, although not really first-rate. There is something about a solid white shirt that conveys honesty, intelligence, and stability; it should be your first choice. It is true that artists, writers, engineers, and other creative types are sometimes known to object to white shirts; for them pale blue may be the best option. Remember that the paler and more subtle the shade, the better the impression you will make.

While monograms are common enough in this country, those who don't accept them usually feel strongly about the implied ostentation of stylized initials on clothing. If you can avoid it, don't take the chance of giving your interviewer the chance to find fault in this area. (On the other hand, if your choice is between wearing your monogrammed shirt or pulling out the old Motley Crue tee-shirt, then your choice should be clear, and so should your conscience.)

Cotton shirts look better and hold up under perspiration more impressively than their synthetic counterparts; if at all possible, opt for a cotton shirt that's been professionally cleaned and starched. A cotton and polyester blend can be an acceptable alternative, but keep in mind that the higher the cotton content, the better the shirt will look. While these blend shirts wrinkle less easily, you are advised to ignore the "wash-and-wear-no-need-to-iron" claims you'll read on the front of the package when you purchase them. Experience has shown that *any* shirt you wear to an interview must be ironed and starched by a professional.

Men's Neckwear: Ties

While an expensive suit can be ruined by a cheap-looking tie, the right tie can do a lot to pull the less-than-perfect suit together for a professional look. When you can't afford a new suit for the interview, you can upgrade your whole look with the right tie.

A pure silk tie makes the most powerful professional impact, has the best finish and feel, and is easiest to tie well. Linen ties are too informal, wrinkle too easily, and may only be worn during warmer weather. (What's more, they can only be tied once between cleanings because they wrinkle so easily.) A wool tie is casual in appearance and has knot problems. Man-made fibers are shiny, make colors look harsh when you want them to look subtle, and may undercut your professional image. A pure silk tie, or a 50-50 wool and silk blend (which is almost wrinkle-proof), should be your choice for the interview.

The tie should complement your suit. This means that there should be a physical balance: the rule of thumb is that the width of your tie should approximate the width of your lapels. The prevailing standard, which has held good for over a decade now, is that ties can range in width between 2¾" and 3½". Wearing anything wider may mark you as someone still trapped in the disco era.

While the tie should complement the suit, it should not *match* it. You would never, for instance, wear a navy blue tie with a navy blue suit. Choose an appropriate tie that neither vanishes into nor does battle with your suit pattern; the most popular and safest styles are found within the categories of solids, foulards, stripes, and paisleys.

Do not wear ties with large polka dots, pictures of animals such as leaping trout or soaring mallards, or sporting symbols such as golf clubs or (God forbid) little men on polo ponies. Never wear any piece of apparel that has a manufacturer's symbol emblazoned on the front as part of the decoration. It is difficult to project an image of competent, balanced professionalism when you are acting as a walking billboard for some fashion designer.

Other considerations include the length of the tie (it should, when tied, extend to your trouser belt), the size of the knot (smaller is better), and whether you should wear a bow tie to an interview (you shouldn't).

Men's Shoes

Shoes should be either black leather or brown leather. Stay away from all other materials and colors: they are too risky.

Lace-up wing tips are the most conservative choice and are almost universally acceptable. Slightly less conservative, but equally appropriate, are slip-on dress shoes—not to be confused with boating shoes. The slip-on, with its low, plain vamp or tassel, is versatile enough to be used for both day and evening business wear. (The lace-up wing tip can look a bit cloddish at dinner.)

In certain areas of the South, Southwest, and West, heeled cowboy boots are not at all unusual for business wear, as are those Grand Ole Opry versions of the business suit. But beware: outside of such specifically defined areas, you will attract only puzzled stares—and few if any professional career opportunities—with these wardrobe selections.

Men's Socks

Socks should complement the suit; accordingly, they are likely to be blue, black, gray, or brown. They should also be long enough for you to cross your legs without showing off lots of bare shin, and should not fall in a bunch toward the ankle as you move. Elastic-reinforced over-the-calf socks are your best bet.

Men's Accessories

The right accessories can enhance the professional image of any applicant, male or female; the wrong accessories can destroy it.

The guiding principle here is to include nothing that could conceivably be misconstrued or leave a bad impression. Never, for instance, should you wear religious or political insignias in the form of rings, ties, or pins. If you would not initiate a conversation about such topics at a job interview (and you shouldn't), why send smoke signals asking your interviewer to do so?

The watch you wear should be simple and plain. This means Mickey Mouse is out, as are sports-oriented and Swatch style watches. No one is impressed by digital watches these days; don't be afraid to wear a simple analog model with a leather strap. (Besides, you don't want people wondering whether you can really tell time, do you?) Avoid cheap-looking pseudo-gold watchbands at all costs.

Your briefcase, if you carry one, can make a strong professional statement about you. Leather makes the best impression, while all other materials follow far behind. Brown and burgundy are the colors of choice. The case itself should be plain, although some very expensive models offer a host of embellishments that only detract from the effect you want.

A cotton or linen handkerchief should be part of every job hunter's wardrobe. Plain white is best. Your handkerchief can also be used to relieve the clammy-hands syndrome so common before the interview. Anything to avoid the infamous "wet fish" handshake!

(By the way, avoid the matching-tie-and-pocket-square look at all costs. It's hideous and inappropriate for a professional interview.)

Belts should match or complement the shoes you select. Accordingly, a blue, black, or gray suit will require a black belt and black shoes, while brown, tan, or beige suits will call for brown. With regard to materials, stick with plain leather. The most common mistake made with belts is the buckle: an interview is not the place for your favorite Harley Davidson, Grateful Dead, or Bart Simpson buckle. Select a small, simple buckle that doesn't overwhelm the rest of your look.

Jewelry

Men may wear a wedding band, if applicable, and a small pair of subdued cufflinks (if wearing French cuffs, of course). Anything more is dangerous. Even fraternity rings—much less bracelets, neck chains, or medallions—can send the wrong message.

Overcoats

The safest and most utilitarian colors for overcoats are beige and blue; stick to these two exclusively. If you can avoid wearing an overcoat, do so (it's an encumbrance and adds to clutter).

Makeup

It is inadvisable for a man to wear makeup to an interview or at any other time during his professional life.

Women

Following are the best current dress guidelines for women preparing for a professional interview.

Women's Suits

You have more room for creativity in this area than men do, but also more room for mistakes. Of course, your creativity must stay within certain accepted guidelines created not by me, nor even by the fashion industry, but by the consensus of the business world. And that is a world, alas, that tends to trail behind the rest of us, and so the options for imaginative masterstrokes are limited.

Limit your creativity to materials, patterns, and cuts. A woman's business wardrobe need no longer be simply a pseudo-male selection of drab grey skirts and blouses. (Recent advice that women should avoid pinstripes or ties is probably insecure and dated. With the right cuts, pinstripes and ties can look both stylish and professional.)

Wool and linen are both accepted as the right look for professional women's suits, but there is a problem. Linen wrinkles so quickly that you may feel as though you leave the house dressed for success, but arrive at your destination destined for bag-ladyhood. Cotton-polyester blends are great for warm climates: they look like linen, but lack the "wrinklability" factor.

Combinations of synthetics and natural fabrics do have their advantages: suits made of such material will certainly retain their shape better. The eye trained to pay attention to detail (read: your interviewers') may well detect the type of fabric, say a cheap polyester blend, and draw unwarranted conclusions about your personality and taste. The choice is up to you; if you do opt for natural fabrics, you will probably want to stay with wool. It provides the smartest look of all, and is most versatile and rugged.

While men are usually limited to either solid or pinstripe suits, a woman can add to this list the varied category of plaids. The Prince of Wales plaid, for instance, is attractive, and is utterly acceptable for businesswomen (no doubt because of its regal namesake).

How long a skirt should you wear? Any hard-and-fast rule I could offer here would be in danger of being outdated almost immediately, as the fashion industry demands dramatically different looks every season in order to fuel sales. (After all, keeping the same hemlines would mean that last season's clothes could last another season or two.)

It should go without saying that you don't want to sport something that soars to the upper thigh if you want to be taken seriously as an applicant. Your best bet is to dress somewhat more conservatively than you would if you were simply showing up for work at the organization in question. Hemlines come and go, and while there is some leeway as to what is appropriate for everyday wear on the job, the safest bet is usually to select something that falls just a little below the knee.

Colors most suitable for interview suits include charcoal, medium gray, steel gray, black, and navy blue. All of these look smart with a white blouse. A navy suit can also look good with a gray or beige blouse (but see the notes on blouse color selection below). You may be tempted to select a burgundy blouse with that navy blue outfit, but save it for a dinner date; it is inappropriate at an interview. In the second tier come beige, tan, and camel suits; these look best with white blouses.

Of all these looks, the cleanest and most professional is the simple solid gray suit (either medium or charcoal) with a white blouse.

Blouses

With regard to blouses, long sleeves will project the authoritative, professional look you desire. Three-quarter length sleeves are less desirable, and they are followed in turn by short sleeves. *Never* wear a sleeveless blouse to an interview. (You may be confident that there is absolutely no chance that you will be required to remove your jacket, but why take the risk?)

Solid colors and natural fabrics (particularly cotton and silk) are the best selections for blouses. Combinations of natural and synthetic fabrics, while wrinkle-resistant, do not absorb moisture well.

The acceptable color spectrum is wider for blouses than for men's shirts, but it is not limitless. The most prudent choices are still white or pale blue; these offer a universal professional appeal. Pink and gray may also be suitable in certain situations (say, at a "creative" company such as an advertising firm for pink, or at an investment bank in a metropolitan area for gray).

The blouse with a front tie bow is most acceptable; it always works well with a suit. Asymmetrical closing blouses, as well as those with the bow at the side, are also good choices for a job interview. The button-down collar always looks great; the more conservative the company/industry, the more positive its impression will be.

Women's Neckwear: Scarves

While a woman might choose to wear a string of pearls instead of a scarf to an interview, the scarf can still serve as a powerful status symbol.

Just as you would expect, a good outfit can be ruined by a cheap-looking scarf. Opting to wear a scarf means that the scarf will be saying something dramatic about you: make sure it's something dramatically positive.

A pure silk scarf will offer a conservative look, a good finish, and ease in tying. Some of the better synthetic blends achieve an overall effect that is almost as good.

While some books on women's clothing will recommend buying blouses that have matching scarves attached to the collar, there is an increasingly vocal lobby of stylish businesswomen who feel this is the equivalent of mandating that a man wear a clip-on bow tie. As with men's ties, the objective is to complement the outfit, not match it. Avoid overly flamboyant styles, and stick with the basics: solids, foulards, small polka dots, or paisleys.

Women's Shoes

Female applicants have a greater color selection in footwear than do their male counterparts. The shoes should still be of leather, but in addition to brown and black a woman is safe in wearing navy, burgundy, black, or even, if circumstances warrant, red.

It is safest to stay away from faddish or multicolored shoes (even such classics as two-toned oxfords). There are two reasons for this: first, all fashion is transitory, and even if you are up-to-date, you cannot assume that your interviewer is; and second, many interviewers are male, and thus are likely to exhibit a notorious inability to appreciate vivid color combinations. As with the rest of your wardrobe, stay away from radical choices, and opt for the easily comprehensible professional look.

Heel height is important, as well. Flats are fine; a shoe with a heel of up to about 1½" is perfectly acceptable. Stay away from high heels: at best you will wobble slightly, and at worst you will walk at an angle. Unless you're an Olympic ski jumper, it's hard to maintain an "in-control" image when you are tipped forward at a forty-five degree angle!

The pump or court shoe, with its closed toe and heel, is perhaps the safest and most conservative look. A closed heel with a slightly open toe is acceptable, too, as is the sling-back shoe with a closed toe.

Stockings or Pantyhose

These should not make a statement of their own. Select neutral skintones in most cases. You may be an exception if you are interviewing for a job in the fashion industry, in which case you might coordinate colors with your outfit, but be very sure of the company standard already in place. Even in such an instance, avoid loud or glitzy looks. A bold black, of course, is out entirely.

Pantyhose and stockings are prone to developing runs at the worst possible moment. Keep an extra pair in your purse or briefcase.

Accessories

Because a briefcase is a symbol of authority, it is an excellent choice for the female applicant. Do not, however, bring both your purse and a briefcase to the interview. (You'll look awkward juggling them around.) Instead, transfer essential items to a small clutch bag you can store in the case. In addition to brown and burgundy (recommended colors for the men), you may include blue and black as possible colors for your case, which should be free of expensive and distracting embellishments.

With regard to belts, the advice given for men holds for women as well. Belts should match or complement the shoes you select; a blue, black, or grey suit will require a black belt and black shoes, while brown, tan, or beige suits will call for brown. In addition, women may wear snakeskin, lizard, and the like. Remember that the belt is a functional item; if it is instantly noticeable, it is wrong.

Jewelry

As far as jewelry goes, less is more. A woman should restrict rings to engagement or wedding bands if these are applicable, but she can wear a necklace and earrings, as long as these are subdued and professional-looking. (I should note that some men are put off by earrings of any description in the workplace, so if you wear them keep them small, discreet, and in good taste. Avoid fake or strangely colored pearls, anything with your name or initials on it, and earrings that dangle or jangle.) In addition, a single bracelet on the woman's wrist is acceptable; anything around the ankle is not. Remember, too much of the wrong kind of jewelry can keep a woman from receiving an offer she might otherwise receive, or inhibit her promotional opportunities once on the team.

Makeup

Take care never to appear overly made-up. Eye makeup should be subtle, so as not to overwhelm the rest of the face. I advise against lipstick at an interview because it does cause negative reactions in some interviewers, and because it will smudge and wear off as the hours wear on. Who can say, going in, how long the meeting will last?

For Men and Women: A Note on Personal Hygiene

It should go without saying that bad breath, dandruff, body odor, and dirty nails have the potential to undo all your efforts at putting across a good first impression. These and related problems denote an underlying professional slovenliness, which an interviewer will feel is likely to reflect itself in your work. You want to show yourself to be appealing, self-respecting, and enjoyable to be around. You can't do that if the people you meet with have to call on exceptional powers of self-control in order to stay in the same room with you.

Don't ask yourself whether any friend or colleague has actually come out and suggested that you pay more attention to these matters; ask yourself how you felt the last time *you* had to conduct business of any sort with a person who had a hygiene problem. Then resolve never to leave that kind of impression.

10.
Body Language

Given the choice of going blind or going deaf, which would you choose?

If you are like nine out of ten other people, you would choose to go deaf. The vast majority of us rely to a remarkable degree on our ability to gather information visually. This really is not all that surprising: while speech is a comparatively recent development, humans have been sending and receiving nonverbal signals from the dawn of the species.

In fact, body language is one of the earliest methods of communication we learn after birth. We master the spoken word later in life, and in so doing we forget the importance of nonverbal cues. But the signals are still sent and received (usually at a subconscious level), even if most of us discount their importance.

It is common to hear people say of the body language they use, "Take me or leave me as I am." This is all very well if you have no concern for what others think of you. For those seeking professional employment, however, it is of paramount importance that the correct body language be utilized. If your mouth says "Hire me," but your body says something quite different, you are likely to leave the interviewer confused. "Well," he or she will think, "the right answers all came out, but there was something about that candidate that just rubbed me the wrong way." Such misgivings are generally sufficient to keep any candidate from making the short list.

When we are in stressful situations (and a job interview is certainly right there in Stress Hell), our bodies react accordingly. The way they react can send unintentional negative messages. The interviewer may or may not be aware of what causes the concern, but the messages will be sent, and our cause will suffer.

Of course, interviewers can be expected to listen carefully to what we say, too. When our body language doesn't contradict our statements, we will generally be given credence. When our body language complements our verbal statements, our message will gain a great deal of impact. But when our body language *contradicts* what we say, it is human nature for the interviewer to be skeptical. In short, learning to control negative body movements during an interview—and learning to use positive body signals—will greatly increase the chances for job interview success.

Under the Microscope

What is the interviewer watching us for during the interview? The answer is: clues. The mystery for the interviewer is, what kind of an employee would we make? It is incumbent on us to provide not just any old clues, but the ones most likely to prompt a decision to hire.

Let's begin at the beginning. When we are invited in to an interview, we are probably safe in assuming that our interviewer believes we meet certain minimum standards, and could conceivably be hired. (Otherwise, why take the time to interview?) Once in the door, we can assume that we will be scrutinized in three main areas:

- Ability (Can we do the job?)
- Willingness (Will we do the job?)
- Manageability (Will we be a pleasure or a pain to have around?)

Appropriate control and use of our gestures can help us emphasize positive features of our personality in these key areas—and also project integrity, honesty, attention to detail, and the like.

The old adage that actions speak louder than words appears to be something we should take quite literally. Studies done at the University of Chicago found that over 50% of all effective communication relies on body language. Since we can expect interviewers to respond to the body language we employ at the interview, it is up to us to decide what messages we want them to receive.

There are also studies that suggest that the impression we create in the first few minutes of the interview are the most lasting. Since the first few minutes after we meet the interviewer is a time when he or she is doing the vast majority of the talking, we have very little control over the impression we create with our words: we can't say much of anything! It is up to our bodies, then, to do the job for us.

The Greeting

Giving a "dead fish" handshake will not advance one's candidacy; neither will the opposite extreme, the iron-man bonecrusher grip.

The ideal handshake starts before the meeting actually occurs. Creating the right impression with the handshake is a three-step process. Be sure that:

1) Your hands are clean and adequately manicured.

2) Your hands are warm and reasonably free of perspiration. (There are a number of ways to ensure this, including washing hands in warm water at the interview site, holding one's hand close to the cheek for a few seconds, and even applying a little talcum powder.)

3) The handshake itself is executed professionally and politely, with a firm grip and a warm smile.

Remember that if you initiate the handshake, you may send the message that you have a desire to dominate the interview; this is not a good impression to leave with one's potential boss. Better to wait a moment and allow the interviewer to initiate the shake. (If for any reason you do find yourself initiating the handshake, do not pull back; if you do, you will appear indecisive. Instead, make the best of it, smile confidently, and make good eye contact.)

The handshake should signal cooperation and friendliness. Match the pressure extended by the interviewer—never exceed it. Ideally, the handshake should last for between three and five seconds, and should "pump" for no more than six times. (The parting handshake may last a little longer. Smile and lean forward very slightly as you shake hands before departing.)

Certain cultural and professional differences should be considered with regard to handshakes, as well. Many doctors, artists, and others who do delicate work with their hands can and do give less enthusiastic handshakes than other people. Similarly, the English handshake is considerably less firm than the American, while the German variety is more firm.

Use only one hand; always shake vertically. Do not extend your hand parallel to the floor, with the palm up, as this conveys submissiveness. By the same token, you may be seen as being too aggressive if you extend your flat hand outward with the palm facing down.

Taking Your Seat

> Some thirty inches from my nose
> The frontier of my person goes.
> Beware of rudely crossing it;
> I have no gun, but I can spit.
> (With apologies to W.H. Auden.)

Encroaching on another's "personal zone" is a bad idea in any business situation, but it is particularly dangerous in an interview. The thirty-inch standard is a good one to follow: it is the distance that allows you to extend your hand comfortably for a handshake. Maintain this distance throughout the interview, and be particularly watchful of intrusions during the early stages when you meet, greet, and take a seat.

Applying this principle may seem simple enough, but how often have you found yourself dodging awkwardly in front of someone to take a seat before it has been offered? A person's office is an extension of sorts of his personal zone; this is why it is not only polite, but also sound business sense, to wait until the interviewer offers you a seat.

It is not uncommon to meet with an interviewer in a conference room or other supposedly "neutral" site. Again, wait for the interviewer to motion you to a spot, or, if you feel uncomfortable doing this, tactfully ask the interviewer to take the initiative: "Where would you like me to sit?"

Facial/Head Signals

Once you take your seat, you can expect the interviewer to do most of the talking. You can also probably expect your nervousness to be at its height. Accordingly, you must be particularly careful about the nonverbal messages you send at this stage.

Now, while all parts of the body are capable of sending positive and negative signals, the head (including the eyes and mouth) is under closest scrutiny. Most good interviewers will make an effort to establish and maintain eye contact, and thus you should expect that whatever messages you are sending from the facial region will be picked up, at least on a subliminal level.

Our language is full of expressions testifying to the powerful influence of facial signals. When we say that someone is shifty-eyed, is tight-lipped, has a furrowed brow, flashes bedroom eyes, stares into space, or grins like a Cheshire cat, we are speaking in a kind of shorthand, and using a set of stereotypes that enables us to make judgments—consciously or unconsciously—about the person's abilities and qualities. Those judgments may not be accurate, but they are usually difficult to reverse.

Tight smiles and tension in the facial muscles often bespeak an inability to handle stress; little eye contact can communicate a desire to hide something; pursed lips are often associated with a secretive nature; and frowning, looking sideways, or peering over one's glasses can send signals of haughtiness and arrogance. Hardly the stuff of which winning interviews are made!

The Eyes

Looking at someone means showing interest in that person, and showing interest is a giant step forward in making the right impression. (Remember, each of us is our own favorite subject!)

Your aim should be to stay with a calm, steady, and non-threatening gaze. It is easy to mismanage this, and so you may have to practice a bit to overcome the common hurdles in this area. Looking away from the interviewer for long periods while he is talking, closing the eyes while being addressed, repeatedly shifting focus from the subject to some other point: these are likely to leave the wrong impression.

Of course, there is a big difference between looking and staring at someone! Rather than looking the speaker straight-on at all times, create a mental triangle incorporating both eyes and the mouth; your eyes will follow a natural, continuous path along the three points. Maintain this approach for roughly three-quarters of the time; you can break your gaze to look at the interviewer's hands as points are emphasized, or to refer to your note pad. These techniques will allow you to leave the impression that you are attentive, sincere, and committed. Staring will only send the message that you are aggressive or belligerent.

Be wary of breaking eye contact too abruptly, and of shifting your focus in ways that will disrupt the atmosphere of professionalism. Examining the interviewer below the head and shoulders, for instance, is a sign of overfamiliarity. (This is an especially important point to keep in mind when being interviewed by someone of the opposite sex.)

The eyebrows send messages as well. Under stress, one's brows may wrinkle; as we have seen, this sends a negative signal about our ability to handle challenges in the business world. The best advice on this score is simply to take a deep breath and collect yourself. Most of the tension that people feel at interviews has to do with anxiety about how to respond to what the interviewer will ask. As a reader of *Knock 'em Dead*, you are prepared, and have credible responses for even the toughest queries. Relax.

The Head

Rapidly nodding your head can leave the impression that you are impatient and eager to add something to the conversation—if only the interviewer would let you. Slower nodding, on the other hand, emphasizes interest, shows that you are validating the comments of your interviewer, and subtly encourages him to continue.

Tilting the head slightly, when combined with eye contact and a natural smile, demonstrates friendliness and approachability. The tilt should be momentary and not exaggerated, almost like a bob of the head to one side. (Do not overuse this technique!)

The Mouth

One guiding principle of good body language is to turn upward rather than downward. Look at two boxers after a fight: the loser is slumped forward, brows knit and eyes downcast, while the winner's smiling face is thrust upward and outward. The victor's arms are raised high, his back is straight, his shoulders are square. In the first instance the signals we receive are those of anger, frustration, belligerence, and defeat; in the second, happiness, openness, warmth, and confidence.

Your smile is one of the most powerful positive body signals in your arsenal; it best exemplifies the up-is-best principle, as well. Offer an unforced, confident smile as frequently as opportunity and circumstances dictate. *Avoid at all costs* the technique some applicants use: grinning idiotically for the length of the interview, no matter what. This will only communicate that you are either insincere or not quite on the right track.

It's worth remembering that the mouth provides a seemingly limitless supply of opportunities to convey weakness. This may be done by touching the mouth frequently (and, typically, unconsciously); "faking" a cough when confronted with a difficult question; and/or gnawing on one's lips absentmindedly. Employing any of these "insincerity signs" when you are asked about, say, why you lost your last job, will confirm or instill suspicions about your honesty and effectiveness.

Glasses

Those who wear glasses sometimes leave them off when going on an interview in an attempt to project a more favorable image. There are two main difficulties with this. The first is that farsighted people who don't wear their glasses will (unwittingly) seem to stare long and hard at the people they converse with, and this, as we have seen, is a negative signal. The second problem is that leaving the glasses at home—even if you replace them with contacts—will actually undercut your cause in most cases. Many studies have shown that those who wear glasses are perceived as being more intelligent than those who don't. Why not take advantage of this effect? The issue is really not *whether* you should wear your glasses—you should—but how best to make them work for you.

Peering over the top of your glasses—even if you wear reading glasses and have been handed something to read and subsequently asked a question—carries professorial connotations that are frequently interpreted as critical. (If you wear glasses for reading, you should remove them when conversing, replacing them only when appropriate.)

Wearing dark glasses to an interview will paint you as secretive, cold, and devious. Even if your prescription glasses are tinted, the effect will be the same. Try to obtain non-tinted glasses for your interview; if you are unable to do so, you are likely to be faced with the only case where contacts are preferable to spectacles.

Body-Signal Barricades

Folding or crossing the arms, or holding things in front of the body, is a wonderful way to send negative messages to the interviewer. The signal is, essentially, "I know you're there, but you can't come in. I'm nervous and closed for business."

It is bad enough to feel this way, but worse to express it with blatant signals. Don't fold your arms or "protect" your chest with hands, clipboard, briefcase, or anything else during the interview. (These positions, in fact, should be avoided in any and every business situation.)

Hands

As we have seen, a confident and positive handshake breaks the ice and gets the interview moving in the right direction. Proper use of the hands throughout the rest of the interview will help to convey an above-board, "nothing-to-hide" message.

Watch out for hands and fingers that take on a life of their own, fidgeting with themselves or other objects such as pens, paper, or your hair. Pen tapping is interpreted as the action of an impatient person; this is an example of an otherwise trivial habit that can take on immense significance in an interview situation. (Rarely will an interviewer ask you to stop doing something annoying; instead, he'll simply make a mental note that you are an annoying person, and congratulate himself for picking this up before making the mistake of hiring you.)

Negative hand messages are legion. Some of the most dangerous are listed below.

- You can demonstrate smugness and superiority by clasping your hands behind your head. (You'll also expose any perspiration marks that are under your arms.)

- A man can show insecurity by simply adjusting his tie, and that's not the worst of it: when interviewing with a woman, his gesture will show something other than a businesslike interest in the interviewer.

- Slouching in your chair, with hands in pockets or thumbs in belt, can brand you as insolent and aggressive—and when this error is made in the presence of an interviewer of the opposite sex, it carries sexually aggressive overtones as well. (Beware, too, of sending these signals while you are walking on a tour of the facility.)

- Pulling your collar away from your neck for a moment may seem like an innocent enough reaction to the heat of the day, but the interviewer might assume that you are tense and/or masking an untruth. (The same goes for scratching the neck during, before, or after your response to a question.)

- Moving the hands toward a feature one perceives as deficient is a common unconscious reaction to stress. A man with thinning hair, for example, may thoughtlessly put his hand to his forehead when pondering how to respond to the query, "Why aren't you earning more at your age?" This habit may be extremely difficult for you to detect in the first place, much less reverse, but make the effort. Such protective movements are likely to be perceived—if only on a subliminal level—as acknowledgments of low status.

- Picking at invisible bits of fluff on one's suit looks like what it is: a nervous tic. Keep your focus on the interviewer. (If you do have some bit of lint somewhere on your clothing, the best advice is usually to ignore it rather than call attention to it by brushing it away.)

By contrast, employing the hands in a positive way can further your candidacy. Here are some of the best techniques.

- Subtly exposing your palms now and then as you speak can help to demonstrate that you are open, friendly, and have nothing to hide. (The technique is used to great effect by many politicians and television talk show hosts; watch for it.)

- When considering a question, it can sometimes be beneficial to "steeple" your fingers for a few seconds as you think and when you first start to talk. Unless you hold the gesture for long periods of time, it will be perceived as a neutral demonstration of your thoughtfulness.

(Of course, if you overuse this or hold the position for too long, you may be taken as condescending.) Steepling will also give you something constructive to do with your hands; it offers a change from holding your pad and pen.

Seating

The signals you send with your body during an interview can be affected by the type of chair you sit in. If you have a choice, go with an upright chair with arms. Deep armchairs can restrict your ability to send certain positive signals, and encourage the likelihood of negative ones. (They're best suited for watching television, not for projecting the image of a competent professional.)

There is only one way to sit during an interview; bottom well back in the chair and back straight. Slouching, of course, is out, but a slight forward leaning posture will show interest and friendliness toward the interviewer. Keep your hands on the sides of the chair; if there are no arms on the chair, keep your hands in your lap or on your pad of paper.

Crossed legs, in all their many forms, send a mixture of signals; most of them are negative.

- Crossing one ankle over the other knee can show a certain stubborn and recalcitrant outlook (as well as the bottom of your shoe, which is not always a pretty sight). The negative signal is intensified when you grasp the horizontally crossed leg or—worst of all—cross your arms across your chest.

- Crossed ankles have often been assumed to indicate that the person doing the crossing is withholding information. However, some dress fashions encourage decorous ankle crossing. Of course, since the majority of interviews take place across a desk, crossed ankles will often be virtually unnoticeable. The best advice on this body signal is that it is probably the most permissible barrier you can erect; if you must allow yourself one body language vice, this is the one to choose.

- When sitting in armchairs or on sofas, crossing the legs may be necessary to create some stability amid all the plush upholstery. In this instance, the signals you send by crossing your legs will be neutral, as long as your crossed legs point toward, rather than away from, the interviewer.

Feet

Some foot signals can have negative connotations. Women and men wearing slip-on shoes should beware of dangling the loose shoe from the toes; this can be quite distracting and, as it is a gesture often used to signal physical attraction, it has no place in a job interview. Likewise, avoid compulsive jabbing of floor, desk, or chair with your foot; this can be perceived as a hostile and angry motion, and is likely to annoy the interviewer.

Walking

Many interviews will require that you walk from point A to point B with the interviewer, either on a guided tour of facilities or to move from one office to another. (Of course, if you are interviewing in a restaurant, you will have to walk with your interviewer to and from the dining facility.) How long these walks last is not as important as how you use them to reinforce positive traits and impressions.

Posture is the first concern. Keep your shoulders back, maintain an erect posture, smile, and make eye contact when appropriate. Avoid fidgeting with your feet as you move, rubbing one shoe against the other, or kicking absentmindedly at the ground as you stand: these signals will lead others to believe that you are anxious and/or insecure.

Crossing your arms or legs while standing carries the same negative connotations as it does when you are sitting. Putting your hands in your pockets is less offensive—assuming you don't jangle keys or coins—but men must be careful not to employ the hands-on-hips or thumbs-in-belt postures discussed earlier. These send messages that you are aggressive and dominating.

Seven Signals For Success

So far we have focused primarily on the pitfalls to avoid; but what messages *should* be sent, and how? Here are seven general suggestions on good body language for the interview.

1) Walk slowly, deliberately, and tall upon entering the room.

2) On greeting your interviewer, give (and, hopefully, receive) a friendly "eyebrow flash": that brief, slight raising of the brows that calls attention to the face, encourages eye contact, and (when accompanied by a natural smile) sends a strong positive signal that that interview has gotten off to a good start.

3) Use mirroring techniques. In other words, make an effort—subtly!—to reproduce the positive signals your interviewer sends. (Of course, you should never mirror negative body signals.) Say the interviewer leans forward to make a point; a few moments later, you lean forward slightly in order to hear better. Say the interviewer leans back and laughs; you "laugh beneath" the interviewer's laughter, taking care not to overwhelm your partner by using an inappropriate volume level. This technique may seem contrived at first, but you will learn that it is far from that, if only you experiment a little.

4) Maintain a naturally alert head position; keep your head up and your eyes front at all times.

5) Remember to avert your gaze from time to time so as to avoid the impression that you are staring; when you do so, look confidently and calmly to the right or to the left; never look down.

6) Do not hurry any movement.

7) Relax with every breath.

Putting It All Together

We have discussed the individual gestures that can either improve or diminish your chances of success at the interview. Working in our favor is the fact that positive signals reinforce one another; employing them in combination yields an overwhelming positive message that is truly greater than the sum of its parts. Now it is time to look at how to combine the various positive elements to send a message of competence and professionalism.

Here is the best posture to aim for during the interview.

- Sit well back in the chair; allow the back of it to support you and help you sit upright. Increase the impression of openness ("I have nothing to hide!") by unbuttoning your jacket as you sit down. Keep your head up. Maintain eye contact a good portion of the time, especially when the interviewer begins to speak and when you reply. Smile naturally whenever the opportunity arises. Avoid folding your arms; it is better to keep them on the arms of your chair. Remember to show one or both of your palms occasionally as you make points, but do not overuse this gesture.

Open for Business

The more open your body movements during the interview, the more you will be perceived as open yourself. Understanding and directing your body language will give you added power to turn interviews into cooperative exchanges between two professionals.

Just as you interpret the body language of others, both positive and negative, so your body language makes an indelible impression on those you meet. It tells them whether you like and have confidence in yourself, whether or not you are pleasant to be around, and whether you are more likely to be honest or deceitful. Like it or not, our bodies carry these messages for the world to see.

Job interviews are reliable in one constant: they bring out insecurities in those who must undergo them. All the more reason to consciously manage the impressions the body sends!

11.
The Curtain Goes Up

Backstage in the theater, the announcement "Places, please" is made five minutes before the curtain goes up. It's the performers' signal to psyche themselves up, complete final costume adjustments, and make time to reach the stage. They are getting ready to go on stage and knock 'em dead. You should go through a similar process.

Winning that job offer depends not only on the things you do well, but also on the absence of things you do poorly. As the interview date approaches, settle down with your resume and the exercises you performed in building it. Immerse yourself in your past successes and strengths. This is a time for building confidence. A little nervousness is perfectly natural and healthy, but channel the extra energy in a positive direction by beginning your physical and mental preparations.

First, you should assemble your interview kit.

- **The company dossier.** — documents about company.

- **Two or three copies of your resume and executive briefing, all but one set for the interviewer.** It is perfectly all right to have your resume in front of you at the interview; it shows that you are organized. It also makes a great cheat sheet (after all, the interviewer is using it for that reason)— you can keep it on your lap during the interview with pad and pencil. It is not unusual to hear, "Mr. Jones wasn't hired because he didn't pay attention to detail and could not even remember his employment dates." And those are just the kinds of things you are likely to forget in the heat of the moment.

- **A pad of paper and writing instruments.** These articles have a twofold purpose. They demonstrate your organization and interest in the job; they also give you something constructive to do with your hands during the interview. Bring along a blue or black ballpoint for filling out applications.

- **Contact telephone numbers.** If you get detained on the way to the interview, you can call and let the company representative know.

- **Reference letters.** Take the sensible precaution of gathering these from your employers, on the off-chance they are requested.

- **A list of job-related questions.** During the interview is the time when you gather information to evaluate a job (the actual evaluation comes when you have an offer in hand). At the end of the interview, you will be given the opportunity to ask additional questions. Develop some that help you understand the job's parameters and potential.

  You might ask: "Why is the job open?" "Where does the job lead?" "What is the job's relationship to other departments?" "How do the job and the department relate to the corporate mission?"

For a longer list of questions that might be valuable to ask along those lines, see Chapter 21, "Negotiating the Offer." Understand, though, that some of those will obviously only be appropriate in the context of a serious negotiation talk. You can also find good questions to ask in the answer to "Do you have any questions?" on page 105.

- **Any additional information you have about the company or the job.** If time permits, ask the interviewer's secretary to send you some company literature. Absorb whatever you can.

- **Directions to the interview.** Decide on your form of transportation and finalize your time of departure. Check the route, distance, and travel time. Write it all down legibly and put it with the rest of your interview kit. If you forget to verify date, time, and place (including floor and suite number), you might not even arrive at the right place, or on the right day, for your interview.

□ □ □

First impressions are the strongest you make, and they are based on your appearance. There is only one way to dress for the first meeting: clean-cut and conservative. You may or may not see yourself that way, but how you see yourself is not important now—your only concern is how others see you. As you could be asked to appear for an interview at a scant couple of hours notice, you must be in a constant state of readiness. Keep your best two suits of clothing freshly cleaned, your shirts or blouses wrinkle-free, and your shoes polished. Never wear these outfits unless you are interviewing.

Here are some more tips:

- Regardless of sex or hairstyle, take it to the lawn doctor once a month.

- While a shower or bath prior to an interview is most desirable, and the use of an unscented deodorant advisable, the wearing of after-shave or perfume should be avoided. You are trying to get hired, not dated.

- You should never drink alcohol the day before an interview. It affects eyes, skin pallor, and your wits.

- Nails should be trimmed and manicured at all times, even if you work with your hands.

□ □ □

To arrive at an interview too early indicates over-anxiousness; to arrive late is inconsiderate. The only sensible solution is to arrive at the interview on time, but at the location early. That allows you time to visit the restroom and make the necessary adjustments to your appearance. Take a couple of minutes in this temporary sanctuary to perform your final mental preparations:

- Review the company dossier.

- Recall the positive things you will say about past employers.

- Breathe deeply and slowly for a minute. This will dispel your natural physical tension.

- Repeat to yourself that the interview will be a success and afterwards the company representatives will wonder how they ever managed without you.

- Smile and head for the interview.

Under no circumstances back out because you do not like the receptionist or the look of the office—that would be allowing interview nerves to get the better of you. As you are shown into the office, you are on!

This potential new employer wants an aggressive and dynamic employee, but someone who is less aggressive and dynamic than he or she is, so take your lead from the interviewer.

Do:

- give a firm handshake—one shake is enough;

- make eye contact and smile. Say, "Hello, Ms. Smith. I am John Jones. I have been looking forward to meeting you."

Do not:

- use first names (unless asked);

- smoke (even if invited);

- sit down (until invited);

- show anxiety or boredom;

- look at your watch;

- discuss equal rights, sex, race, national origin, religion, or age;

- show samples of your work (unless requested);

- ask about benefits, salary, or vacation;

- assume a submissive role. Treat the interviewer with respect, but as an equal.

Now you are ready for anything. Except for the tough questions that are going to be thrown at you next.

III

Great Answers to Tough Interview Questions

"Like being on trial for your life" is how many people look at a job interview. They are probably right. With the interviewer as judge and jury, you are at least on trial for your livelihood. Therefore, you must lay the foundation for a winning defense. F. Lee Bailey, America's most celebrated defense attorney, attributes his success in the courtroom to preparation. He likens himself to a magician going into court with 50 rabbits in his hat, not knowing which one he'll really need, but ready to pull out any single one. Bailey is successful because he is ready for any eventuality. He takes the time to analyze every situation and every possible option. He never underestimates his opposition. He is always prepared. F. Lee Bailey usually wins.

Another famous attorney, Louis Nizer, successfully defended all of his 50-plus capital offense clients. When lauded as the greatest courtroom performer of his day, Nizer denied the accolade. He claimed for himself the distinction of being the *best prepared*.

You won't win your day in court just based on your skills. As competition for the best jobs increases, employers are comparing more and more applicants for every opening and asking more and more questions. To win against stiff competition, you need more than just your merits. When the race is close, the final winner is often as not picked for a comparative lack of negatives when ranged against the other contenders. Like Bailey and Nizer, you can prove to yourself that the prize always goes to the best prepared.

During an interview, employers ask you dozens of searching questions. Questions that test your confidence, poise, and desirable personality traits. Questions that trick you into contradicting yourself. Questions that probe your quick thinking and job skills. They are all designed so that the interviewer can make decisions in some critical areas:

- Can you do the job?

- Will you complement or disrupt the department?

- Are you willing to take the extra step?

- Are you manageable?

- Is the money right?

Notice that only one of the critical areas has anything to do with your actual job skills. Being able to do the job is only a small part of getting an offer. Whether you will fit in and make a contribution, and whether you are manageable, are just as important to the interviewer. Those traits the company probes for during the interview are the same that will mark a person for professional growth when on board. In this era of high unemployment and high specialization, companies become more critical in the selection process and look more actively for certain traits, some of which cannot be ascertained by a direct question or answer. Consequently, the interviewer will seek a pattern in your replies that shows your possession of such traits—I discuss them in detail in the next chapter.

The time spent in "court" on trial for your livelihood contains four deadly traps:

- your failure to listen to the question;

- annoying the interviewer by answering a question that was not asked;

- providing superfluous information (you should keep answers brief, thorough, and to the point);

- attempting to interview without preparation.

The effect of those blunders is cumulative, and each reduces your chances of receiving a job offer.

The number of offers you win in your search for the ideal job depends on your ability to answer a staggering array of questions in terms that have value and relevance to the employer: "Why do you want to work here?" "What are your biggest accomplishments?" "How long will it take you to make a contribution?" "Why should I hire you?" "What can you do for us that someone else cannot do?" "What is your greatest weakness?" "Why aren't you earning more?" and, "What interests you least about this job?" are just some of the questions you will be asked.

The example answers in the following chapters come from across the job spectrum. Though the example answer might come from the mouth of an administrator, while you are a scientist or in one of the service industries, the commonality of all job functions in contributing to the bottom line will help you draw the parallel to your job.

You will also notice that each of the example answers teaches a small yet valuable lesson in good business behavior—something you can use both to get the job and to make a good impression when you are on board.

And remember, the answers provided in the following chapters should not be repeated word for word, exactly as they come off the page. You have your own style of speech (not to mention your own kind of business experience), so try to put the answers in your own words.

12.
How to
Knock 'em Dead

- "Describe a situation where your work or an idea was criticized."

- "Have you done the best work you are capable of doing?"

- "What problems do you have getting along with others?"

- "How long will you stay with the company?"

- "I'm not sure you're suitable for the job."

- "Tell me about something you are not very proud of."

- "What are some of the things your supervisor did that you disliked?"

- "What aspects of your job do you consider most crucial?"

Can you answer all these questions off the top of your head? Can you do it in a way that will set your worth above the other job candidates? I doubt it—they were *designed* to catch you off guard. But they won't after you have read the rest of *Knock 'em Dead*.

Even if you could answer some of them, it would not be enough to assure you of victory: The employer is looking for certain intangible assets as well. Think back to your last job for a moment. Can you recall someone with fewer skills, less professionalism, and less dedication who somehow leveraged his or her career into a position of superiority to you? He or she was able to do that only by cleverly projecting a series of personality traits that are universally sought by all successful companies. Building those key traits into your answers to the interviewer's questions will win you any job and set the stage for your career growth at the new company.

There are 20 universally admired key personality traits; they are your passport to success at any interview. Use them for reference as you customize your answers to the tough questions in the following chapters.

Personal Profile:

The interviewer searches for personal profile keys to determine what type of person you really are. The presence of these keys in your answers tells the company representative how you feel about yourself, your chosen career, and what you would be like to work with. Few of them will arise from direct questions—your future employer will search for them in your answers to specific job-performance probes. The following words and phrases are those you will project as part of your successful, healthy personal profile.

- **Drive:** A desire to get things done. Goal-oriented.

- **Motivation:** Enthusiasm and a willingness to ask questions. A company realizes that a motivated person accepts added challenges and does that little bit extra on every job.

- **Communication Skills:** More than ever, the ability to talk and write effectively to people at all levels in a company is a key to success.

- **Chemistry:** The company representative is looking for someone who does not get rattled, wears a smile, is confident without self-importance, gets along with others—who is, in short, a team player.

- **Energy:** Someone who always gives that extra effort in the little things as well as important matters.

- **Determination:** Someone who does not back off when a problem or situation gets tough.

- **Confidence:** Not braggadocio. Poise. Friendly, honest, and open to employees high or low. Not intimidated by the big enchiladas, nor overly familiar.

Professional Profile:

All companies seek employees who respect their profession and employer. Projecting these professional traits will identify you as loyal, reliable, and trustworthy.

- **Reliability:** Following up on yourself, not relying on anyone else to ensure the job is well done, and keeping management informed every step of the way.

- **Honesty/Integrity:** Taking responsibility for your actions, both good and bad. Always making decisions in the best interests of the company, never on whim or personal preference.

- **Pride:** Pride in a job well done. Always taking the extra step to make sure the job is done to the best of your ability. Paying attention to the details.

- **Dedication:** Whatever it takes in time and effort to see a project through to completion, on deadline.

- **Analytical Skills:** Weighing the pros and cons. Not jumping at the first solution to a problem that presents itself. The short- and long-term benefits of a solution against all its possible negatives.

- **Listening Skills:** Listening and understanding, as opposed to waiting your turn to speak.

Achievement Profile:

Earlier, I discussed that companies have very limited interests: making money, saving money (the same as making money), and saving time (which does both). Projecting your achievement profile, in however humble a fashion, is the key to winning any job.

- **Money Saved:** Every penny saved by your thought and efficiency is a penny earned for the company.

- **Time Saved:** Every moment saved by your thought and efficiency enables your company to save money and make more in the additional time available. Double bonus.

- **Money Earned:** Generating revenue is the goal of every company.

Business Profile:

Projecting your business profile is important on those occasions when you cannot demonstrate ways you have made money, saved money, or saved time for previous employers. These keys demonstrate you are always on the lookout for opportunities to contribute, and that you keep your boss informed when an opportunity arises.

- **Efficiency:** Always keeping an eye open for wastage of time, effort, resources, and money.

- **Economy:** Most problems have two solutions: an expensive one, and one the company would prefer to implement.

- **Procedures:** Procedures exist to keep the company profitable. Don't work around them. That also means keeping your boss informed. You tell your boss about problems or good ideas, not his or her boss. Follow the chain of command. Do not implement your own "improved" procedures or organize others to do so.

- **Profit:** The reason all the above traits are so universally admired in the business world is because they relate to profit.

As the requirements of the job are unfolded for you at the interview, meet them point by point with your qualifications. If your experience is limited, stress the appropriate key profile traits (such as energy, determination, motivation), your relevant interests, and your desire to learn. If you are weak in just one particular area, keep your mouth shut—perhaps that dimension will not arise. If the area is probed, be prepared to handle and overcome the negative by stressing skills that compensate and/or demonstrate that you will experience a fast learning curve.

Do not show discouragement if the interview appears to be going poorly. You have nothing to gain by showing defeat, and it could merely be a stress interview tactic to test your self-confidence.

If for any reason you get flustered or lost, keep a straight face and posture; gain time to marshal your thoughts by asking, "Could you help me with that?" or, "Would you run that by me again?" or, "That's a good question; I want to be sure I understand. Could you please explain it again?"

Now it is time for you to study the tough questions. Use the examples and explanations to build answers that reflect your background and promote your skills and attributes.

"What are the reasons for your success in this profession?"

With this question, the interviewer is not so much interested in examples of your success—he or she wants to know what makes you tick. Keep your answers short, general, and to the point. Using your work experience, personalize and use value keys from your personal, professional and business profiles. For example: "I attribute my success to three reasons: the support I've always received from co-workers, which always encourages me to be cooperative and look at my specific job in terms of what we as a department are trying to achieve. That gives me great pride in my work and its contribution to the department's efforts. Finally, I find that every job has its problems that need solutions, and while there's always a costly solution, there's usually an economical one as well, whether it's in terms of time or money." Then give an example from your experience that illustrates those points.

"What is your energy level like? Describe a typical day."

You must demonstrate good use of your time, that you believe in planning your day beforehand, and that when it is over, you review your own performance to make sure you are reaching the desired goals. No one wants a part-time employee, so you should sell your energy level. For example, your answer might end with: "At the end of the day when I'm ready to go home, I make a rule always to type one more letter [make one more call, etc.] and clear my desk for the next day."

"Why do you want to work here?"

To answer this question, you must have researched the company and built a dossier. Your research work from Chapter 1 is now rewarded. Reply with the company's attributes as you see them. Cap your answer with reference to your belief that the company can provide you with a stable and happy work environment—the company has that reputation—and that such an atmosphere would encourage your best work.

"I'm not looking for just another paycheck. I enjoy my work and am proud of my profession. Your company produces a superior product/provides a superior service. I share the values that make this possible, which should enable me to fit in and complement the team."

"What kind of experience do you have for this job?"

This is a golden opportunity to sell yourself, but before you do, be sure you know what is most critical to the interviewer. The interviewer is not just looking for a competent engineer, typist, or what-have-you—he or she is looking for someone who can contribute quickly to the current projects. When interviewing, companies invariably give everyone a broad picture of the job, but the person they hire will be a problem-solver, someone who can contribute to the specific projects in the first six months. Only by asking will you identify the areas of your interviewer's greatest urgency and therefore interest.

If you do not know the projects you will be involved with in the first six months, you must ask. Level-headedness and analytical ability are respected, and the information you get will naturally let you answer the question more appropriately. For example, a company experiencing shipping problems might appreciate this answer: "My high-speed machining background and familiarity with your equipment will allow me to contribute quickly. I understand deadlines, delivery schedules, and the importance of getting the product shipped. Finally, my awareness of economy and profit has always kept reject parts to a bare minimum."

"What are the broad responsibilities of a [e.g.] systems analyst?"

This is suddenly becoming a very popular question with interviewers, and rightly so. There are three layers to it. First, it acknowledges that all employees nowadays are required to be more efficiency- and profit-conscious, and need to know how individual responsibilities fit into the big picture. Second, the answer provides some idea of how much you will have to be taught or re-oriented if and when you join the company. Third, it is a very effective knock-out question—if you lack a comprehensive understanding of your job, that's it! You'll be knocked out then and there.

While your answer must reflect an understanding of the responsibilities, be wary of falling afoul of differing corporate jargon. A systems analyst in one company, for instance, may be only a programmer trainee in another. With that in mind, you may wish to preface your answer with, "While the responsibilities of my job title vary somewhat from company to company, at my current/last job, my responsibilities included . . ." Then, in case your background isn't an exact match, ask, "Which areas of relevant expertise haven't I covered?" That will give you the opportunity to recoup.

"Describe how your job relates to the overall goals of your department and company."

This not only probes your understanding of department and corporate missions, but also obliquely checks into your ability to function as a team member to get the work done. Consequently, whatever the specifics of your answer, include words to this effect: "The quality of my work directly affects the ability of others to do their work properly. As a team member, one has to be aware of the other players."

"What aspects of your job do you consider most crucial?"

A wrong answer can knock you out of the running in short order. The executive who describes expense reports as the job's most crucial aspect is a case in point. The question is designed to determine time management, prioritization skills, and any inclination for task avoidance.

"Are you willing to go where the company sends you?"

Unfortunately with this one, you are, as the saying goes, damned if you do and damned if you don't. What is the real question? Do they want you to relocate or just travel on business? If you simply answer "no," you will not get the job offer, but if you answer "yes," you could end up in Monkey's Eyebrow, Kentucky. So play for time and ask, "Are you talking about business travel, or is the company relocating?" In the final analysis, your answer should be "yes." You don't have to accept the job, but without the offer you have no decision to make. Your single goal at an interview is to sell yourself and win a job offer. Never forget, only when you have the offer is there a decision to make about that particular job.

"What did you like/dislike about your last job?"

The interviewer is looking for incompatibilities. If a trial lawyer says he or she dislikes arguing a point with colleagues, such a statement will only weaken—if not immediately destroy—his or her candidacy.

Most interviews start with a preamble by the interviewer about the company. Pay attention: That information will help you answer the question. In fact, any statement the interviewer makes about the job or corporation can be used to your advantage.

So, in answer, you liked everything about your last job. You might even say your company taught you the importance of certain keys from the business, achievement, or professional profile. Criticizing a prior employer is a warning flag that you could be a problem employee. No one intentionally hires trouble, and that's what's behind the question. Keep your answer short and positive. You are allowed only one negative about past employers, and only then if your interviewer has a "hot button" about his or her department or company; if so, you will have written it down on your notepad. For example, the only thing your past employer could not offer might be something like "the ability to contribute more in different areas in the smaller environment you have here." You might continue with, "I really liked everything about the job. The reason I want to leave it is to find a position where I can make a greater contribution. You see, I work for a large company that encourages specialization of skills. The smaller environment you have here will, as I said, allow me to contribute far more in different areas." Tell them what they want to hear—replay the hot button.

Of course, if you interview with a large company, turn it around. "I work for a small company and don't get the time to specialize in one or two major areas." Then replay the hot button.

"What is the least relevant job you have held?"

If your least relevant job is not on your resume, it shouldn't be mentioned. Some people skip over those six months between jobs when they worked as soda jerks just to pay the bills, and would rather not talk about it, until they hear a question like this one. But a mention of a job that, according to all chronological records, you never had, will throw your integrity into question and your candidacy out the door.

Apart from that, no job in your profession has been a waste of time if it increases your knowledge about how the business works and makes money. Your answer will include: "Every job I've held has given me new insights into my profession, and the higher one climbs, the more important the understanding of the lower-level, more menial jobs. They all play a role in making the company profitable. And anyway, it's certainly easier to schedule and plan work when you have first-hand knowledge of what others will have to do to complete their tasks."

"What have you learned from jobs you have held?"

Tie your answer to your business and professional profile. The interviewer needs to understand that you seek and can accept constructive advice, and that your business decisions are based on the ultimate good of the company, not your personal whim or preference. "More than anything, I have learned that what is good for the company is good for me. So I listen very carefully to directions and always keep my boss informed of my actions."

"How do you feel about your progress to date?"

This question is not geared solely to rate your progress; it also rates your self-esteem (personal profile keys). Be positive, yet do not give the impression you have already done your best work. Make the interviewer believe you see each day as an opportunity to learn and contribute, and that you see the environment at this company as conducive to your best efforts.

"Given the parameters of my job, my progress has been excellent. I know the work, and I am just reaching that point in my career when I can make significant contributions."

"Have you done the best work you are capable of doing?"

Say "yes," and the interviewer will think you're a has-been. As with all these questions, personalize your work history. For this particular question, include the essence of this reply: "I'm proud of my professional achievements to date, especially [give an example]. But I believe the best is yet to come. I am always motivated to give my best efforts, and in this job there are always opportunities to contribute when you stay alert."

"How long would you stay with the company?"

The interviewer might be thinking of offering you a job. So you must encourage him or her to sell you on the job. With a tricky question like this, end your answer with a question of your own that really puts the ball back in the interviewer's court. Your reply might be: "I would really like to settle down with this company. I take direction well and love to learn. As long as I am growing professionally, there is no reason for me to make a move. How long do you think I would be challenged here?"

"How long would it take you to make a contribution to our company?"

Again, be sure to qualify the question: In what area does the interviewer need rapid contributions? You are best advised to answer this with a question: "That is an excellent question. To help me answer, what do you anticipate my responsibilities will be for the first six or seven months?" or, "What are your greatest areas of need right now?" You give yourself time to think while the interviewer concentrates on images of you working for the company. When your time comes to answer, start with: "Let's say I started on Monday the 17th. It will take me a few weeks to settle down and learn the ropes. I'll be earning my keep very quickly, but making a real contribution . . . [give a hesitant pause] Do you have a special project in mind you will want me to get involved with?" That response could lead directly to a job offer, but if not, you already have the interviewer thinking of you as an employee.

"What would you like to be doing five years from now?"

The safest answer contains a desire to be regarded as a true professional and team player. As far as promotion, that depends on finding a manager with whom you can grow. Of course, you will ask what opportunities exist within the company before being any more specific: "From my research and what you have told me about the growth here, it seems operations is where the heavy emphasis is going to be. It seems that's where you need the effort and where I could contribute toward the company's goals." Or, "I have always felt that first-hand knowledge and experience open up opportunities that one might never have considered, so while at this point in time I plan to be a part of [e.g.] operations, it is reasonable to expect that other exciting opportunities will crop up in the meantime."

"What are your qualifications?"

Be sure you don't answer the wrong question. Does the interviewer want job-related or academic job qualifications? Ask. If the question concerns job-related information, you need to know what problems must be tackled first before you can answer adequately. If you can determine this, you will also know what is causing the manager most concern. Then, if you can show yourself as someone who can contribute to the solution of those projects/problems, you have taken a dramatic step ahead in the race for the job offer. Ask for clarification, then use appropriate value keys from all four categories tied in with relevant skills and achievements. You might say: "I can give you a general answer, but I feel my answer might be more valuable if you could tell me about specific work assignments in the early months."

Or: "If the major task right now is to automate the filing system, I should tell you that in my last job I was responsible for creating a computerized database for a previously uncomputerized firm."

"What are your biggest accomplishments?"

Keep your answers job related; from earlier exercises, a number of achievements should spring to mind. If you exaggerate contributions to major projects, you will be accused of suffering from "coffee-machine syndrome," the affliction of a junior clerk who claimed success for an Apollo space mission based on his relationships with certain scientists, established at the coffee machine. You might begin your reply with: "Although I feel my biggest achievements are still ahead of me, I am proud of my involvement with . . . I made my contribution as part of that team and learned a lot in the process. We did it with hard work, concentration, and an eye for the bottom line."

"How do you organize and plan for major projects?"

Effective planning requires both forward thinking ("Who and what am I going to need to get this job done?") and backward thinking ("If this job must be completed by the 20th, what steps must be made, and at what time, to achieve it?"). Effective planning also includes contingencies and budgets for time and cost overruns. Show that you cover all the bases.

"How many hours a week do you find it necessary to work to get your job done?"

No absolutely correct answer here, so again, you have to cover all the bases. Some managers pride themselves on working nights and weekends, or on never taking their full vacation quota. Others pride themselves on their excellent planning and time management that allows them never to work more than regular office hours. You must pick the best of both worlds: "I try to plan my time effectively and usually can. Our business always has its rushes, though, so I put in whatever effort it takes to get the job finished." It is rare that the interviewer will then come back and ask for a specific number of hours. If that does happen, turn the question around: "It depends on the projects. What is typical in your department?" The answer will give you the right cue, of course.

"Tell me how you moved up through the organization."

A fast-track question, the answer to which tells a lot about your personality, your goals, your past, your future, and whether you still have any steam left in you. The answer might be long, but try to avoid rambling. Include a fair sprinkling of your key personality traits in your stories (because this is the perfect time to do it). As well as listing the promotions, you will want to demonstrate that they came as a result of dedicated, long-term effort, substantial contributions, and flashes of genius.

"Can you work under pressure?"

You might be tempted to give a simple yes or no answer, but don't. It reveals nothing, and you lose the opportunity to sell your skills and value profiles. Actually, this common question often comes from an unskilled interviewer, because it is closed-ended. (How to handle different types of interviewers is covered in Chapter 14, "The Other Side of the Desk.") As such, the question does not give you the chance to elaborate. Whenever you are asked a closed-ended question, mentally add: "Please give me a brief yet comprehensive answer." Do that, and you will give the information requested and seize an opportunity to sell yourself. For example, you could say: "Yes, I usually find it stimulating. However, I believe in planning and proper management of my time to reduce panic deadlines within my area of responsibility."

"What is your greatest strength?"

Isolate high points from your background and build in a couple of the key value profiles from different categories. You will want to demonstrate pride, reliability, and the ability to stick with a difficult task yet change course rapidly when required. You can rearrange the previous answer here. Your answer in part might be: "I believe in planning and proper management of my time. And yet I can still work under pressure."

"What are your outstanding qualities?"

This is essentially the same as an interviewer asking you what your greatest strengths are. While in the former question you might choose to pay attention to job-specific skills, this question asks you to talk about your personality profile. Now while you are fortunate enough to have a list of the business world's most desirable personality traits at the beginning of this chapter, try to do more than just list them. In fact, rather than offering a long "laundry list," you might consider picking out just two or three and giving an illustration of each.

"What interests you most about this job?"

Be straightforward, unless you haven't been given adequate information to determine an answer, in which case you should ask a question of your own to clarify. Perhaps you could say, "Before answering, could I ask you to you tell me a little more about the role this job plays in the departmental goals?" or, "Where is the biggest vacuum in your department at the moment?" or, "Could you describe a typical day for me?" The additional information you gather with those questions provides the appropriate slant to your answer—that is, what is of greatest benefit to the department and to the company. Career-wise, that obviously has the greatest benefit to you, too. Your answer then displays the personality traits that support the existing need. Your answer in part might include, "I'm looking for a challenge and an opportunity to make a contribution, so if you feel the biggest challenge in the department is _____, I'm the one for the job." Then include the personality traits and experience that support your statements. Perhaps: "I like a challenge, my background demonstrates excellent problem-solving abilities [give some examples], and I always see a project through to the finish."

"What are you looking for in your next job?"

You want a company where your personal profile keys and professional profile keys will allow you to contribute to business value keys. Avoid saying what you want the company to give you; you must say what you want in terms of what you can give to your employer. The key word in the following example is "contribution": "My experience at the XYZ Corporation has shown me I have a talent for motivating people. That is demonstrated by my team's absenteeism dropping 20 percent, turnover steadying at 10 percent, and production increasing 12 percent. I am looking for an opportunity to continue that kind of contribution, and a company and supervisor who will help me develop in a professional manner."

"Why should I hire you?"

Your answer will be short and to the point. It will highlight areas from your background that relate to current needs and problems. Recap the interviewer's description of the job, meeting it point by point with your skills. Finish your answer with: "I have the qualifications you need [itemize them], I'm a team player, I take direction, and I have the desire to make a thorough success."

"What can you do for us that someone else cannot do?"

This question will come only after a full explanation of the job has been given. If not, qualify the question with: "What voids are you trying to eradicate when you fill this position?" Then recap the interviewer's job description, followed with: "I can bring to this job a determination to see projects through to a proper conclusion. I listen and take direction well. I am analytical and don't jump to conclusions. And finally, I understand we are in business to make a profit, so I keep an eye on cost and return." End with: "How do these qualifications fit your needs?" or, "What else are you looking for?"

You finish with a question that asks for feedback or a powerful answer. If you haven't covered the interviewer's hot buttons, he or she will cover them now, and you can respond accordingly.

"Describe a difficult problem you've had to deal with."

This is a favorite tough question. It is not so much the difficult problem that's important—it's the approach you take to solving problems in general. It is designed to probe your professional profile; specifically, your analytical skills.

"Well, I always follow a five-step format with a difficult problem. One, I stand back and examine the problem. Two, I recognize the problem as the symptom of other, perhaps hidden, factors. Three, I make a list of possible solutions to the problem. Four, I weigh both the consequences and cost of each solution, and determine the best solution. And five, I go to my boss, outline the problem, make my recommendation, and ask for my superior's advice and approval."

Then give an example of a problem and your solution. Here is a thorough example: "When I joined my present company, I filled the shoes of a manager who had been fired. Turnover was very high. My job was to reduce turnover and increase performance. Sales of our new copier had slumped for the fourth quarter in a row, partly due to ineffective customer service. The new employer was very concerned, and he even gave me permission to clean house. The cause of the problem? The customer-service team never had any training. All my people needed was some intensive training. My boss gave me permission to join the American Society for Training and Development, which cost $120. With what I learned there, I turned the department around. Sales continued to slump in my first quarter. Then they skyrocketed. Management was pleased with the sales and felt my job in customer service had played a real part in the turnaround; my boss was pleased because the solution was effective and cheap. I only had to replace two customer-service people."

"What would your references say?"

You have nothing to lose by being positive. If you demonstrate how well you and your boss got along, the interviewer does not have to ask, "What do you dislike about your current manager?"

It is a good idea to ask past employers to give you a letter of recommendation. That way, you know what is being said. It reduces the chances of the company representative checking up on you, and if you are asked this question you can pull out a sheaf of rousing accolades and hand them over. If your references are checked by the company, it must by law have your written permission. That permission is usually included in the application form you sign. All that said, never offer references or written recommendations unless they are requested.

"Can we check your references?"

This question is frequently asked as a stress question to catch the too-smooth candidate off guard. It is also one that occasionally is asked in the general course of events. Very few managers or companies ever check references—that astounds me, yet it's a fact of life. On the other hand, the higher up the corporate ladder you go, the more likely it is that your references will be checked.

There is only one answer to this question if you ever expect to get an offer: "Yes."

Your answer may include: "Yes, of course you can check my references. However, at present, I would like to keep matters confidential, until we have established a serious mutual interest [i.e., an offer]. At such time I will be pleased to furnish you with whatever references you need from prior employers. I would expect you to wait to check my current employer's references until you have extended an offer in writing, I have accepted, we have agreed upon a start date, and I have had the opportunity to resign in a professional manner." You are under no obligation to give references of a current employer until you have a written offer in hand. You are also well within your rights to request that reference checks of current employers wait until you have started your new job.

"What type of decisions did you make on your last job?"

Your answer should include reference to the fact that your decisions were all based on appropriate business profile keys. The interviewer may be searching to define your responsibilities, or he or she may want to know that you don't overstep yourself. It is also an opportunity, however humble your position, to show your achievement profile.

For example: "Being in charge of the mailroom, my job is to make sure people get information in a timely manner. The job is well defined, and my decisions aren't that difficult. I noticed a year or two ago that when I took the mail around at 10 a.m., everything stopped for 20 minutes. I had an idea and gave it to my boss. She got it cleared by the president, and ever since, we take the mail around just before lunch. Mr. Gray, the president, told me my idea improved productivity and saved time, and that he wished everyone was as conscientious."

"What was the last book you read (or movie you saw)? How did it affect you?"

It doesn't really matter what you say about the latest book/movie, just as long as you have read/seen it. Don't be like the interviewee who said the name of the first book that came to mind—*In Search of Excellence*—only to be caught by the follow-up, "To what extent do you agree with Peters' simultaneous loose/tight pronouncements?" Also, by naming such a well known book, you have managed only to say that you are like millions of others, which doesn't make you stand out in the crowd. Better that you should name something less faddish—that helps to avoid nasty follow-up questions. And you needn't mention the most *recent* book or movie you've seen. Your answer must simply make a statement about you as a potential employee. Come up with a response that will set you apart and demonstrate your obvious superiority. Ideally you want to mention a work that in some way has helped you improve yourself; anything that has honed any of the 20 key personality traits will do.

"How do you handle tension?"

This question is different from "Can you handle pressure?"–it asks *how* you handle it. You could reply, "Tension is caused when you let things pile up. It is usually caused by letting other areas of responsibility slip by for an extended period. For instance, if you have a difficult presentation coming up, you may procrastinate in your preparations for it. I've seen lots of people do things like that—a task seems so overwhelming they don't know where to begin. I find that if you break those overwhelming tasks into little pieces, they aren't so overwhelming any more. So I suppose I don't so much handle tension as handle the causes of it, by not letting things slip in other areas that can give rise to it."

"How long have you been looking for another position?"

If you are employed, your answer isn't that important—a short or long time is irrelevant to you in any follow-up probes, because you are just looking for the right job, with the right people and outfit that offers you the right opportunities. If, on the other hand, you are unemployed at the time of the question, how you answer becomes more important. If you say, "Well, I've been looking for two years now," it isn't going to score you any points. The interviewer thinks, "Two years, huh? And no one else wanted him in that time. I wonder what's wrong with him? Well, if no one else is interested, I'm certainly not." So if you must talk of months or more be careful to add something like, "Well, I've been looking for about a year now. I've had a number of offers in that time, but I have determined that as I spend most of my waking hours at work, the job I take and the people I work with have got to be people with values I can identify with. I made the decision that I just wasn't going to suffer clock-watchers and work-to-rule specialists anymore."

"Have you ever been fired?"

Say "no" if you can; if not, act on the advice given to the next question.

"Why were you fired?"

If you were laid off as part of general workforce reduction, be straightforward and move on to the next topic as quickly as possible. If you have been terminated with cause, however, this is a very difficult question to answer. Like it or not, termination with cause is usually justified, because the most loathed responsibility of any manager is to take away someone's livelihood. Virtually no one fires an employee for the heck of it.

Looking at that painful event objectively, you will probably find the cause of your dismissal rooted in the absence of one or more of the 20 profiles. Having been fired also creates instant doubt in the mind of the interviewer, and greatly increases the chances of your references being checked. So if you have been fired, the first thing to do is bite the bullet and call the person who fired you, find out why it happened, and learn what he or she would say about you today.

Your aim is to clear the air, so whatever you do, don't be antagonistic. Reintroduce yourself, explain that you are looking (or, if you have been unemployed for a while, say you are "still looking") for a new job. Say that you appreciate that the manager had to do what was done, and that you learned from the experience. Then ask, "If you were asked as part of a pre- or post-employment reference check, how would you describe my leaving the company? Would you say that I was fired or that I simply resigned? You see, every time I tell someone about my termination, whoosh, there goes another chance of getting another paycheck!" Most managers will plump for the latter option (describing your departure as a resignation). After all, even testy managers tend to be humane after the fact, and such a response saves them potential headaches and even lawsuits.

Whatever you do, don't advertise the fact you were fired. If you are asked, be honest, but make sure you have packaged the reason in the best light possible. Perhaps: "I'm sorry to say, but I deserved it. I was having some personal problems at the time, and I let them affect my work. I was late to work and lost my motivation. My supervisor (whom, by the way, I still speak to) had directions to trim the workforce anyway, and as I was hired only a couple of years ago, I was one of the first to go."

If you can find out the employee turnover figures, voluntary or otherwise, you might add: "Fifteen other people have left so far this year." A combination answer of this nature minimizes the stigma. You have even managed to demonstrate that you take responsibility for your actions, which shows your analytical and listening skills. If one of your past managers will speak well of you, there is nothing to lose and everything to gain by finishing with: "Jill Johnson, at the company, would be a good person to check for a reference on what I have told you."

I would never advise you to be anything but honest in your answers to any interview question. If, however, you have been terminated by a manager who is still vindictive, take heart: Only about 10 percent of all successful job candidates ever get their references checked.

"Have you ever been asked to resign?"

When someone is asked to resign, it is a gesture on the part of the employer: "You can quit, or we will can you, so which do you want it to be?" Because you were given the option, though, that employer cannot later say, "I had to ask him to resign"—that is tantamount to firing and could lead to legal problems. In the final analysis, it is safe to answer "no."

"Were you ever dismissed from your job for a reason that seemed unjustified?"

Another sneaky way of asking, "Were you ever fired?" The sympathetic phrasing is geared to getting you to reveal all the sordid details. The cold hard facts are that hardly anyone is ever fired without cause, and you're kidding yourself if you think otherwise. With that in mind, you can quite honestly say, "No," and move on to the next topic.

"In your last job, what were some of the things you spent most of your time on, and why?"

Employees come in two categories: goal-oriented (those who want to get the job done), and task-oriented (those who believe in "busy" work). You must demonstrate good time management, and that you are, therefore, goal-oriented, for that is what this question probes.

You might reply: "I work on the telephone like a lot of businesspeople; meetings also take up a great deal of time. What is more important to me is effective time management. I find more gets achieved in a shorter time if a meeting is scheduled, say, immediately before lunch or at the close of business. I try to block my time in the morning. At four o'clock, I review what I've achieved, what went right or wrong, and plan adjustments and my main thrust of business for tomorrow."

"In what ways has your job prepared you to take on greater responsibility?"
This is one of the most important questions you will have to answer. The interviewer is looking for examples of your professional development, perhaps to judge your future growth potential, so you must tell a story that demonstrates it. The following example shows growth, listening skills, honesty, and adherence to procedures. Parts of it can be adapted to your personal experience. Notice the then-and-now aspect of the answer.

"When I first started my last job, my boss would brief me morning and evening. I made some mistakes, learned a lot, and got the jobs in on time. As time went by I took on greater responsibilities, [list some of them]. Nowadays, I meet with her every Monday for breakfast to discuss any major directional changes, so that she can keep management informed. I think that demonstrates not only my growth, but also the confidence my management has in my judgment and ability to perform consistently above standard."

"In what ways has your job changed since you originally joined the company?"
You can use the same answer here as for the previous question.

"How does this job compare with others you have applied for?"
This is a variation of more direct questions, such as, "How many other jobs have you applied for?" and "Who else have you applied to?" but it is a slightly more intelligent question and therefore more dangerous. It asks you to compare. Answer the question and sidestep at the same time.

"No two jobs are the same, and this one is certainly unlike any other I have applied for." If you are pressed further, say, "Well, to give you a more detailed answer, I would need to ask you a number of questions about the job and the company. Would now be a good time to do that or would it be better later in the interview process?"

"What makes this job different from your current/last one?"
If you don't have enough information to answer the question, say so, and ask some of your own. Behind the question is the interviewer's desire to uncover experience you are lacking—your answer could be used as evidence against you. Focus on the positive: "From what I know of the job, I seem to have all the experience required to make a thorough success. I would say that the major differences seem to be . . ." and here you play back the positive attributes of the department and company as the interviewer gave them to you, either in the course of the interview or in answer to your specific questions.

"Do you have any questions?"

A good question. Almost always, this is a sign that the interview is drawing to a close, and that you have one more chance to make an impression. Remember the old adage: People respect what you inspect, not what you expect. Create questions from any of the following.

- Find out why the job is open, who had it last, and what happened to him or her. Did he or she get promoted or fired? How many people have held this position in the last couple of years? What happened to them subsequently?

- Why did the interviewer join the company? How long has he or she been there? What is it about the company that keeps him or her there?

- To whom would you report? Will you get the opportunity to meet that person?

- Where is the job located? What are the travel requirements, if any?

- What type of training is required, and how long is it? What type of training is available?

- What would your first assignment be?

- What are the realistic chances for growth in the job? Where are the opportunities for greatest growth within the company?

- What are the skills and attributes most needed to get ahead in the company?

- Who will be the company's major competitor over the next few years? How does the interviewer feel the company stacks up against them?

- What has been the growth pattern of the company over the last five years? Is it profitable? How profitable? Is the company privately or publicly held?

- If there is a written job description, may you see it?

- How regularly do performance evaluations occur? What model do they follow?

13.
"What Kind of Person Are You Really, Mr. Jones?"

Will you reduce your new employer's life expectancy? The interviewer wants to know! If you are offered the job and accept, you will be working together 50 weeks of the year. Every employer wants to know whether you will fit in with the rest of the staff, whether you are a team player, and most of all: Are you manageable?

There are a number of questions the interviewer might use to probe this area. They will mainly be geared to your behavior and attitudes in the past. Remember: It is universally believed that your past actions predict your future behavior.

"How do you take direction?"

This is really two questions. "How do you take direction?" and, "How do you take criticism?" Your answer will cover both points. "I take direction well and believe there are two types: carefully explained direction, when my boss has time to treat me with honor and respect; then there is the other, a brusque order or correction. While most people get upset with that, personally I always believe the manager is troubled with bigger problems and a tight schedule. As such, I take the direction and get on with the job without taking offense so my boss can get on with her job. It's the only way."

"Would you like to have your boss' job?"

It is a rare boss who wants his or her livelihood taken. On my very first interview, my future boss said, "Mr. Yate, it has been a pleasure to meet you. However, until you walked in, I wasn't looking for a new job."

By the same token, ambition is admired, but mainly by the ambitious. Be cautiously optimistic. Perhaps: "Well, if my boss were promoted over the coming years, I hope to have made a strong enough contribution to warrant his recommendation. I'm looking for a manager who will help me develop my capabilities and grow with him."

"What do you think of your current/last boss?"

Short, sweet, and shut up. People who complain about their employers are recognized to be the same people who cause the most disruption in a department. This question means the interviewer has no desire to hire trouble. "I liked her as a person, respected her professionally, and appreciated her guidance." The question is often followed by one that tries to validate your answer.

"Describe a situation where your work or an idea was criticized."

A doubly dangerous question. You are being asked to say how you handle criticism and to detail your faults. If you are asked this question, describe a poor idea that was criticized, not poor work. Poor work can cost money and is a warning sign, obviously, to the interviewer.

One of the wonderful things about a new job is that you can leave the past entirely behind, so it does not matter how you handled criticism in the past. What does matter is how the interviewer would like you to handle criticism, if and when it becomes his or her unpleasant duty to dish it out; that's what the question is really about. So relate one of those it-seemed-like-a-good-idea-at-the-time ideas, and finish with how you handled the criticism. You could say: "I listened carefully and resisted the temptation to interrupt or defend myself. Then I fed back what I heard to make sure the facts were straight. I asked for advice, we bounced some ideas around, then I came back later and represented the idea in a more viable format. My supervisor's input was invaluable."

"Tell me about yourself."

This is not an invitation to ramble on. You need to know more about the question before giving an answer. "What area of my background would be most relevant to you?" That enables the interviewer to help you with the appropriate focus, so you can avoid discussing irrelevancies. Never answer this question without qualifying whether the interviewer wishes to hear about your business or personal life.

However the interviewer responds to your qualifying question, the tale you tell should demonstrate one or more of the 20 key personality profiles—perhaps honesty, integrity, being a team player, or determination. If you choose "team player," part of your answer might include this: "I put my heart into everything I do, whether it be sports or work. I find that getting along with your peers and being part of the team makes life more enjoyable and productive."

"Rate yourself on a scale of one to ten."

A stupid question. That aside, bear in mind that this is meant to plumb the depths of your self-esteem. If you answer ten, you run the risk of portraying yourself as insufferable; on the other hand, if you say less than seven, you might as well get up and leave. You are probably best claiming to be an eight or nine, saying that you always give of your best, but that in doing so you always increase your skills and therefore always see room for improvement.

"What kinds of things do you worry about?"

Some questions, such as this one, can seem so off-the-wall that you might start treating the interviewer as a father confessor in no time flat. Your private phobias have nothing to do with your job, and revealing them can get you labeled as unbalanced. It is best to confine your answer to the sensible worries of a conscientious professional. "I worry about deadlines, staff turnover, tardiness, back-up plans for when the computer crashes, or that one of my auditors burns out or defects to the competition—just the normal stuff. It goes with the territory, so I don't let it get me down."

"What is the most difficult situation you have faced?"

The question looks for information on two fronts: How do you define difficult? and, what was your handling of the situation? You must have a story ready for this one in which the situation both was tough and allowed you to show yourself in a good light. Avoid talking about problems that have to do with co-workers. You can talk about the difficult decision to fire someone, but emphasize that once you had examined the problem and reached a conclusion you acted quickly and professionally, with the best interests of the company at heart.

"What are some of the things that bother you?" "What are your pet hates?" "Tell me about the last time you felt anger on the job."

These questions are so similar that they can be treated as one. It is tremendously important that you show you can remain calm. Most of us have seen a colleague lose his or her cool on occasion—not a pretty sight and one that every sensible employer wants to avoid. This question comes up more and more often the higher up the corporate ladder you climb and the more frequent your contact with clients and the general public. To answer it, find something that angers conscientious workers. "I enjoy my work and believe in giving value to my employer. Dealing with clock-watchers and the ones who regularly get sick on Mondays and Fridays really bothers me, but it's not something that gets me angry or anything like that." An answer of this nature will help you much more than the kind given by a California engineer, who went on for some minutes about how he hated the small mindedness of people who don't like pet rabbits in the office.

"What have you done that shows initiative?"

The question probes whether you are a doer, someone who will look for ways to increase sales, save time, or save money—the kind of person who gives a manager a pleasant surprise once in a while, who makes life easier for co-workers. Be sure, however, that your example of initiative does not show a disregard for company policies and procedures.

"My boss has to organize a lot of meetings. That means developing agendas, letting employees around the country know the dates well in advance, getting materials printed, etc. Most people in my position would wait for the work to be given them. I don't. Every quarter, I sit down with my boss and find out the dates of all his meetings for the next six months. I immediately make the hotel and flight arrangements and then work backwards. I ask myself questions like, 'If the agenda for the July meeting is to reach the field at least six weeks before the meeting, when must it be finished by?' Then I come up with a deadline. I do that for all the major activities for all the meetings. I put the deadlines in his diary; and mine, only two weeks earlier. That way I remind the boss that the deadline is getting close. My boss is the best organized, most relaxed manager in the company. None of his colleagues can understand how he does it."

"What are some of the things about which you and your supervisor disagreed?"
It is safest to state that you did not disagree.

"In what areas do you feel your supervisor could have done a better job?"
The same goes for this one. No one admires a Monday-morning quarterback.
You could reply, though: "I have always had the highest respect for my supervisor. I have always been so busy learning from Mr. Jones that I don't think he could have done a better job. He has really brought me to the point where I am ready for greater challenges. That's why I'm here."

"What are some of the things your supervisor did that you disliked?"
If you and the interviewer are both non-smokers, for example, and your boss isn't, use it. Apart from that: "You know, I've never thought of our relationship in terms of like or dislike. I've always thought our role was to get along together and get the job done."

"How well do you feel your boss rated your job performance?"
This is one very sound reason to ask for written evaluations of your work before leaving a company. Some performance-review procedures include a written evaluation of your performance—perhaps your company employs it. If you work for a company that asks you to sign your formal review, you are quite entitled to request a copy of it. You should also ask for a letter of recommendation whenever you leave a job: You have nothing to lose. While I don't recommend thrusting recommendations under unwilling interviewers' noses (they smell a rat when written endorsements of any kind are offered unrequested), the time will come when you are asked and can produce them with a flourish. If you don't have written references, perhaps: "My supervisor always rated my job performance well. In fact, I was always rated as being capable of accepting further responsibilities. The problem was there was nothing available in the company—that's why I'm here."
If your research has been done properly you can also quote verbal appraisals of your performance from prior jobs. "In fact, my boss said only a month ago that I was the most valuable [e.g.] engineer in the workgroup, because . . ."

"How did your boss get the best out of you?"
This is a manageability question, geared to probing whether you are going to be a pain in the neck or not. Whatever you say, it is important for your ongoing happiness that you make it clear you don't appreciate being treated like a dishrag. You can give a short, general answer: "My last boss got superior effort and

performance by treating me like a human being and giving me the same personal respect with which she liked to be treated herself." This book is full of answers that get you out of tight corners and make you shine, but this is one instance in which you really should tell it like it is. You don't want to work for someone who is going to make life miserable for you.

"How interested are you in sports?"

A recently completed survey of middle- and upper-management personnel found that the executives who listed group sports/activities among their extra-curricular activities made an average of $3,000 per year more than their seden-tary colleagues. Don't you just love baseball suddenly? The interviewer is look-ing for your involvement in groups, as a signal that you know how to get along with others and pull together as a team.

"I really enjoy most team sports. Don't get a lot of time to indulge myself, but I am a regular member of my company's softball team." Apart from team sports, endurance sports are seen as a sign of determination: swimming, running, and cycling are all okay. Games of skill (bridge, chess, and the like) demonstrate analytical skills. Being a Grand Master of Dungeons and Dragons doesn't demonstrate a damned thing.

"What personal characteristics are necessary for success in your field?"

You know the answer to this one: It's a brief recital of key personality profiles.

You might say: "To be successful in my field? Drive, motivation, energy, con-fidence, determination, good communication, and analytical skills. Combined, of course, with the ability to work with others."

"Do you prefer working with others or alone?"

This question is usually used to determine whether you are a team player. Before answering, however, be sure you know whether the job requires you to work alone. Then answer appropriately. Perhaps: "I'm quite happy working alone when necessary. I don't need much constant reassurance. But I prefer to work in a group—so much more gets achieved when people pull together."

"Explain your role as a group/team member."

You are being asked to describe yourself as either a team player or a loner. Most departments depend on harmonious teamwork for their success, so describe yourself as a team player, by all means: "I perform my job in a way that helps others to do theirs in an efficient fashion. Beyond the mechanics, we all have a responsibility to make the workplace a friendly and pleasant place to be. That means everyone working for the common good and making the necessary per-sonal sacrifices toward that good."

"How would you define a conducive work atmosphere?"

This is a tricky question, especially because you probably have no idea what kind of work atmosphere exists in that particular office. So, the longer your answer, the greater your chances of saying the wrong thing. Keep it short and sweet. "One where the team has a genuine interest in its work and desire to turn out a good product/deliver a good service."

"Do you make your opinions known when you disagree with the views of your supervisor?"

If you can, state that you come from an environment where input is encouraged when it helps the team's ability to get the job done efficiently. "If opinions are sought in a meeting, I will give mine, although I am careful to be aware of others' feelings. I will never criticize a co-worker or a superior in open forum; besides, it is quite possible to disagree without being disagreeable. However, my past manager made it clear that she valued my opinion by asking for it. So, after a while, if there was something I felt strongly about, I would make an appointment to sit down and discuss it one on one." You might choose to end by turning the tables with a question of your own: "Is this a position where we work as a team to solve problems and get the job done, or one where we are meant to be seen and not heard and speak when spoken to?"

"What would you say about a supervisor who was unfair or difficult to work with?"

For this job, you'll definitely want to meet your potential supervisor—just in case you have been earmarked for the company Genghis Khan without warning. The response, "Do you have anyone in particular in mind?" will probably get you off the hook. If you need to elaborate, try: "I would make an appointment to see the supervisor and diplomatically explain that I felt uncomfortable in our relationship, that I felt he or she was not treating me as a professional colleague, and therefore that I might not be performing up to standard in some way—that I wanted to right matters and ask for his or her input as to what I must do to create a professional relationship. I would enter into the discussion in the frame of mind that we were equally responsible for whatever communication problems existed, and that this wasn't just the manager's problem."

"Do you consider yourself a natural leader or a born follower?"

Ow! How you answer depends a lot on the job offer you are chasing. If you are a recent graduate, you are expected to have high aspirations, so go for it. If you are already on the corporate ladder with some practical experience in the school of hard knocks, you might want to be a little more cagey. Assuming you are up for and want a leadership position, you might try something like this: "I would be reluctant to regard anyone as a natural leader. Hiring, motivating, and disciplining other adults and at the same time molding them into a cohesive team involves a number of delicately tuned skills that no honest people can say they were born with. Leadership requires first of all the desire; then it is a lifetime learning process. Anyone who reckons they have it all under control and has nothing more to learn isn't doing the employer any favors."

Of course, a little humility is also in order, because just about every leader in every company reports to someone, and there is a good chance that you are talking to such a someone right now. So you might consider including something like, "No matter how well developed any individual's leadership qualities, an integral part of the skills of a leader is to take direction both from his or her immediate boss, and also to seek the input of the people being supervised. The wise leader will always follow good advice and sound business judgment wherever it comes from. I would say that given the desire to be a leader, the true leader in the modern business world must embrace both." How can anyone disagree with that kind of wisdom?

"Why do you feel you are a better [e.g.] secretary than some of your co-workers?"
If you speak disparagingly of your co-workers, you will not put yourself in the best light. That is what the question asks you to do, so it poses some difficulties. The trick is to answer the question but not to accept the invitation to show yourself from anything other than a flattering perspective. "I think that question is best answered by a manager. It is so difficult to be objective, and I really don't like to slight my co-workers. I don't spend my time thinking about how superior I am, because that would be detrimental to our working together as a team. I believe, however, some of the qualities that make me an outstanding secretary are . . ." and you go on to illustrate job-related personal qualities that make you a beacon of productivity and a joy to work with.

"You have a doctor's appointment arranged for noon. You've waited two weeks to get in. An urgent meeting is scheduled at the last moment, though. What do you do?"
What a crazy question, you mutter. It's not. It is even more than a question—it is what I call a question shell. The question within the shell—in this instance, "Will you sacrifice the appointment or sacrifice your job?—can be changed at will. This is a situational-interviewing technique, which poses an on-the-job problem to see how the prospective employee will respond. A Chicago company asks this question as part of its initial screening, and if you give the wrong answer, you never even get a face-to-face interview. So what is the right answer to this or any similar shell question?

Fortunately, once you understand the interviewing technique, it is quite easy to handle—all you have to do is turn the question around. "If I were the manager who had to schedule a really important meeting at the last moment, and someone on my staff chose to go to the doctor's instead, how would I feel?"

It is unlikely that you would be an understanding manager unless the visit were for a triple bypass. To answer, you start with an evaluation of the importance of the problem and the responsibility of everyone to make some sacrifices for the organization, and finish with: "The first thing I would do is reschedule the appointment and save the doctor's office inconvenience. Then I would immediately make sure I was properly prepared for the emergency meeting."

"How do you manage to interview while still employed?"
As long as you don't explain that you faked a dentist appointment to make

the interview you should be all right. Beware of revealing anything that might make you appear at all underhanded. Best to make the answer short and sweet and let the interviewer move on to richer areas of inquiry. Just explain that you had some vacation time due, or took a day off in lieu of overtime payments. "I had some vacation time, so I went to my boss and explained I needed a couple of days off for some personal business, and asked her what days would be most suitable. Although I plan to change jobs, I don't in any way want to hurt my current employer in the process by being absent during a crunch."

"When do you expect a promotion?"

Tread warily, show you believe in yourself, and have both feet firmly planted on the ground. "That depends on a few criteria. Of course, I cannot expect promotions without the performance that marks me as deserving of promotion. I also need to join a company that has the growth necessary to provide the opportunity. I hope that my manager believes in promoting from within and will help me grow so that I will have the skills necessary to be considered for promotion when the opportunity comes along."

If you are the only one doing a particular job in the company, or you are in management, you need to build another factor into your answer. For example: "As a manager, I realize that part of my job is to have done my succession planning, and that I must have someone trained and ready to step into my shoes before I can expect to step up. That way I play my part in preserving the chain of command." To avoid being caught off guard with queries about your having achieved that in your present job, you can finish with: "Just as I have done in my present job, where I have a couple of people capable of taking over the reins when I leave."

"Tell me a story."

Wow. What on earth does the interviewer mean by that question? You don't know until you get him or her to elaborate. Ask, "What would you like me to tell you a story about?" To make any other response is to risk making a fool of yourself. Very often the question is asked to see how analytical you are: People who answer the question without qualifying show that they do not think things through carefully. The subsequent question will be about either your personal or professional life. If it is about your personal life, tell a story that shows you like people and are determined. Do not discuss your love life. If the subsequent question is about your professional life, tell a story that demonstrates your willingness and manageability.

"What have your other jobs taught you?"

Talk about the professional skills you have learned and the personality traits you have polished. Many interviewees have had success finishing their answer with: "There are two general things I have learned from past jobs. First, if you are confused, ask—it's better to ask a dumb question than make a stupid mistake. Second, it's better to promise less and produce more than to make unrealistic forecasts."

"Define cooperation."

The question asks you to explain how to function as a team player in the workplace. Your answer could be: "Cooperation is a person's ability to sacrifice personal wishes and beliefs whenever necessary to assure the department reaches its goals. It is also a person's desire to be part of a team, and by hard work and goodwill make the department greater than the sum of its parts."

"What difficulties do you have tolerating people with different backgrounds and interests from yours?"

Another "team player" question with the awkward inference that you do have problems. Give the following answer: "I don't have any."

"In hindsight, what have you done that was a little harebrained?"

You are never harebrained in your business dealings, and you haven't been harebrained in your personal life since graduation, right? The only safe examples to use are ones from your deep past that ultimately turned out well. One of the best to use, if it applies to you, is this one: "Well, I guess the time I bought my house. I had no idea what I was letting myself in for, and at the time, I really couldn't afford it. Still, I managed to make the payments, though I had to work like someone possessed. Yes, my first house—that was a real learning experience." Not only can most people relate to this example, but it also gives you the opportunity to sell one or two of your very positive and endearing traits.

If you think the interview is only tough for the interviewee, it's time to take a look at the other side of the desk. Knowing what's going on behind those Foster Grants can really help you shine.

14.
The Other Side
of the Desk

There are two terrible places to be during an interview—sitting in front of the desk wondering what on earth is going to happen next, and sitting behind the desk asking the questions. The average interviewer dreads the meeting almost as much as the interviewee, yet for opposite reasons.

American business frequently yields to the mistaken belief that any person, on being promoted to the ranks of management, becomes mystically endowed with all necessary managerial skills. That is a fallacy. Comparatively few management people have been taught to interview; most just bumble along and pick up a certain proficiency over a period of time.

There are two distinct types of interviewers who can spell disaster for you if you are unprepared. One is the highly skilled interviewer, who has been trained in systematic techniques for probing your past for all the facts and evaluating your potential. The other is the totally incompetent interviewer, who may even lack the ability to phrase a question adequately. Both are equally dangerous when it comes to winning the job offer.

The Skillful Interviewer

Skillful interviewers know exactly what they want to discover. They have taken exhaustive steps to learn the strategies that will help them hire only the best for their company. They follow a set format for the interview process to ensure objectivity in selection and a set sequence of questions to ensure the facts are gathered. They will definitely test your mettle.

There are many ways for a manager to build and conduct a structured interview, but all have the same goals:

- to ensure a systematic coverage of your work history and applicable job-related skills;

- to provide a technique for gathering all the relevant facts;

- to provide a uniform strategy that objectively evaluates all job candidates;

- to determine ability, willingness, and manageability.

Someone using structured interview techniques will usually follow a standard format. The interview will begin with small talk and a brief introduction to relax you. Following close on the heels of that chit-chat comes a statement geared to assure you that baring your faults is the best way to get the job. Your interviewer will then outline the steps in the interview. That will include you giving a chronological description of your work history, and then the interviewer asking specific questions about your experience. Then, prior to the close of the interview, you will be given an opportunity to ask your own questions.

Sounds pretty simple, huh? Well, watch out! The skilled interviewer knows exactly what questions to ask, why they will be asked, in what order they will be asked, and what the desired responses are. He or she will interview and evaluate every applicant for the job in exactly the same fashion. You are up against a pro.

Like the hunter who learns to think like his or her prey, you will find that the best way to win over the interviewer is to think like the interviewer. In fact, take that idea a little further: You must win, but you don't want the other guys to realize you beat them at their own game. To do that, you must learn how the interviewer has prepared for you; and by going through the same process you will beat out your competitors for the job offer.

The dangerous part of this type of structured interview is called "skills evaluation." The interviewer has analyzed all the different skills it takes to do the job, and all the personality traits that complement those skills. Armed with that data, he or she has developed a series of carefully-sequenced questions to draw out your relative merits and weaknesses.

Graphically, it looks like this:

Letters A-F are the separate skills necessary to do the job; numbers 1-20 are questions asked to identify and verify that particular skill. This is where many of the tough questions will arise, and the only way to prepare effectively is to take the interviewer's viewpoint and complete this exercise in its entirety. It requires a degree of objectivity, but will generate multiple job offers.

☐ Look at the position you seek. What role does it play in helping the company achieve its corporate mission and make a profit?

☐ What are the five most important duties of that job?

☐ From a management viewpoint, what are the skills and attributes necessary to perform each of these tasks?

Write it all down. Now, put yourself in the interviewer's shoes. What topics would you examine to find out whether a person can really do the job? If for some reason you get stuck in the process, just use your past experience. You have worked with good and bad people, and their work habits and skills will lead you to develop both the potential questions and the correct answers.

Each job skill you identify is fertile ground for the interviewer's questions. Don't forget the intangible skills that are so important to many jobs, like self-confidence and creativity, because the interviewer won't. Develop a number of questions for each job skill you identify.

Again, looking back at co-workers (and still wearing the manager's mask), what are the personal characteristics that would make life more comfortable for you as a manager? Those are also dimensions that are likely to be probed by the interviewer. Once you have identified the questions you would ask in the interviewer's position, the answers should come easily.

That's the way managers are trained to develop structured interview questions—I just gave you the inside track. Complete the exercise by developing the answers you would like to hear as a manager. Take time to complete the exercise conscientiously, writing out both the questions and the appropriate answers.

☐☐☐

These sharks have some juicy questions to probe your skills, attitude, and personality. Would you like to hear some of them? Notice that these questions tend to lay out a problem for you to solve, but in no way lead you towards the answer. They are often two- and three-part questions as well. The additional question that can be tagged onto them all is, "What did you learn from this experience?" Assume it is included whenever you get one of these questions—you'll be able to sell different aspects of your success profile.

"You have been given a project that requires you to interact with different levels within the company. How do you do this? What levels are you most comfortable with?"

This is a two-part question that probes communication and self-confidence skills. The first part asks how you interact with superiors and motivate those working with and for you on the project. The second part of the question is saying, "Tell me whom you regard as your peer group—help me categorize you." To cover those bases, you will want to include the essence of this: "There are basically two types of people I would interact with on a project of this nature. First, there are those I report to, who bear the ultimate responsibility for its success. With them, I determine deadlines and how they will evaluate the success of the project. I outline my approach, breaking the project down into component parts, getting approval on both the approach and the costs. I would keep my supervisors up-to-date on a regular basis, and seek input whenever needed. My supervisors would expect three things from me: the facts, an analysis of potential problems, and that I not be intimidated, as that would jeopardize the project's success. I would comfortably satisfy those expectations.

"The other people to interact with on a project like this are those who work with and for me. With those people, I would outline the project and explain how a successful outcome will benefit the company. I would assign the component parts to those best suited to each, and arrange follow-up times to assure completion by deadline. My role here would be to facilitate, motivate, and bring the different personalities together to form a team.

"As for comfort level, I find this type of approach enables me to interact comfortably with all levels and types of people."

"Tell me about an event that really challenged you. How did you meet the challenge? In what way was your approach different from others'?"

This is a straightforward two-part question. The first probes your problem-solving abilities. The second asks you to set yourself apart from the herd. First of all, outline the problem. The blacker you make the situation, the better. Having done that, go ahead and explain your solution, its value to your employer, and how it was different from other approaches.

"My company has offices all around the country; I am responsible for 70 of them. My job is to visit each office on a regular basis and build market-penetration strategies with management, and to train and motivate the sales and customer-service force. When the recession hit, the need to service those offices was more important than ever, yet the traveling costs were getting prohibitive.

"Morale was an especially important factor; you can't let outlying offices feel defeated. I re-apportioned my budget and did the following: I dramatically increased telephone contact with the offices. I instituted a monthly sales-technique letter—how to prospect for new clients, how to negotiate difficult sales, and so forth. I bought and rented sales training and motivational tapes and sent them to my managers with instructions on how to use them in a sales meeting. I stopped visiting all the offices. Instead, I scheduled weekend training meetings in central locations throughout my area: one day of sales training and one day of management training, concentrating on how to run sales meetings, early termination of low producers, and so forth.

"While my colleagues complained about the drop in sales, mine increased, albeit a modest six percent. After two quarters, my approach was officially adopted by the company."

"Give me an example of a method of working you have used. How did you feel about it?"

You have a choice of giving an example of either good or bad work habits. Give a good example, one that demonstrates your understanding of corporate goals, your organizational skills, analytical ability, or time management skills.

You could say: "I believe in giving an honest day's work for a day's pay. That requires organization and time management. I do my paperwork at the end of each day, when I review the day's achievements; with this done, I plan for tomorrow. When I come to work in the morning, I'm ready to get going without wasting time. I try to schedule meetings right before lunch; people get to the point more quickly if it's on their time. I feel that is an efficient and organized method of working."

"When you joined your last company and met the group for the first time, how did you feel? How did you get on with them?"

Your answer should include: "I naturally felt a little nervous, but I was excited about the new job. I shared that excitement with my new friends, and told them that I was enthusiastic about learning new skills from them. I was open and friendly, and when given the opportunity to help someone myself, I jumped at it."

"In your last job, how did you plan to interview?"

That's an easy one. Just give a description of how the skilled interviewer prepares.

"How have you benefited from your disappointments?"

Disappointments are different from failures. It is an intelligent—probably trained—interviewer who asks this one; it is also an opportunity for the astute interviewee to shine. The question itself is very positive—it asks you to show how you benefited. Note also that it doesn't ask you to give specific details of specific disappointments, so you don't have to open your mouth and insert your foot. Instead, be general. Edison once explained his success as an inventor by claiming that he knew more ways not to do something than anyone else living; you can do worse than quote him. In any event, sum up your answer with, "I treat disappointments as a learning experience; I look at what happened, why it happened, and how I would do things differently in each stage should the same set of circumstances appear again. That way, I put disappointment behind me and am ready with renewed vigor and understanding to face the new day's problems."

A side note. A person with strong religious beliefs may be tempted to answer a question like this in terms of religious values. If you benefit from disappointments in a spiritual way, remember that not everyone feels the same as you do. More important, the interviewer is not allowed by law to talk about religion with you, so you can unwittingly put the interviewer in an awkward position of not knowing how to respond. And making an interviewer feel awkward in any way is not the way to win the job offer.

"What would you do when you have a decision to make and no procedure exists?"

This question probes your analytical skills, integrity, and dedication. Most of all, the interviewer is testing your manageability and adherence to procedures—the "company way of doing things." You need to cover that with: "I would act without my manager's direction only if the situation were urgent and my manager were not available. Then, I would take command of the situation, make a decision based on the facts, and implement it. I would update my boss at the earliest opportunity." If possible, tell a story to illustrate.

"That is an excellent answer. Now to give me a balanced view, can you give me an example that didn't work out so well?"

There are two techniques that every skilled interviewer will use, especially if you are giving good answers. In this question, the interviewer looks for negative balance; in the follow-up, the person will look for negative confirmation. Here, you are required to give an example of an inadequacy. The trick is to pull something from the past, not the present, and to finish with what you learned from the experience. For example: "That's easy. When I first joined the workforce, I didn't really understand the importance of systems and procedures. There was one time when I was too anxious to contribute and didn't have the full picture. There was a sales visit report everyone had to fill out after visiting a customer. I always put a lot of effort into it until I realized it was never read; it just went in the files. So I stopped doing it for a few days to see if it made any difference. I thought I was gaining time to make more sales for the company. I was so proud of my extra sales calls I told the boss at the end of the week. My boss explained that the records were for the long term, so that should my job change, the next salesperson would have the benefit of a full client history. It was a long time ago, but I have never forgotten the lesson: There's always a reason for systems and procedures. I've had the best-kept records in the company ever since."

To look for negative confirmation, the interviewer then may say something like, "Thank you. Now can you give me another example?" He or she is trying to confirm a weakness. If you help, you could well do yourself out of a job. Here's your reaction: You sit deep in thought for a good 10 seconds, then look up and say firmly, "No, that's the only occasion when anything like that happened." Shut up and refuse to be enticed further.

The Unconscious Incompetent

Now you should be ready for almost anything a professional interviewer could throw at you. Your foresight and strategic planning will generate multiple offers of employment for you in all circumstances except one, and that's when you face the unconsciously incompetent interviewer. He or she is probably more dangerous to your job-offer status than everything else combined.

The problem is embodied in the experienced manager who is a poor interviewer, but who does not know it. He or she, consciously or otherwise, bases hiring decisions on "experience" and "knowledge of mankind" and "gut feeling." In any event, he or she is an unconscious incompetent. You have probably been interviewed by one in your time. Remember leaving an interview and, upon reflection, feeling the interviewer knew absolutely nothing about you or your skills? If so, you know how frustrating that can be. Here, you'll see how to turn that difficult situation to your advantage. In the future, good managers who are poor interviewers will be offering jobs with far greater frequency than ever before. Understand that a poor interviewer can be a wonderful manager; interviewing skills are learned, not inherited or created as a result of a mystical corporate blessing.

The unconscious incompetents abound. Their heinous crime can only be exceeded by your inability to recognize and take advantage of the proffered opportunity.

As in handling the skilled interviewer, it is necessary to imagine how the unconscious incompetent thinks and feels. There are many manifestations of the poor interviewer. After each of the next examples, follow instructions for appropriate handling of the unique problems each type poses for you.

☐ **Example One:** The interviewer's desk is cluttered, and the resume or application that was handed to him or her a few minutes before cannot be found.

Response: Sit quietly through the bumbling and searching. Check out the surroundings. Breathe deeply and slowly to calm any natural interview nerves. As you bring your adrenaline under control, you bring a certain calming effect to the interviewer and the interview. (This example, by the way, is usually the most common sign of the unconscious incompetent.)

☐ **Example Two:** The interviewer experiences constant interruptions from the telephone or people walking into the office.

Response: This provides good opportunities for selling yourself. Make note on your pad of where you were in the conversation and refresh the interviewer on the point when you start talking again. He or she will be impressed with your level head and good memory. The interruptions also give time, perhaps, to find something of common interest in the office, something you can compliment. You will also have time to compose the suitable value key follow-up to the point made in the conversation prior to the interruption.

☐ **Example Three:** The interviewer starts with an explanation of why you are both sitting there, and then allows the conversation to degenerate into a lengthy diatribe about the company.

Response: Show interest in the company and the conversation. Sit straight, look attentive (the other applicants probably fall asleep), make appreciative murmurs, and nod at the appropriate times until there is a pause. When that occurs, comment that you appreciate the background on the company, because you can now see more clearly how the job fits into the general scheme of things; that you see, for example, how valuable communication skills would be for the job. Could the interviewer please tell you some of the other job requirements? Then, as the job's functions are described, you can interject appropriate information about your background with: "Would it be of value, Mr. Smith, if I described my experience with . . . ?"

☐ **Example Four:** The interviewer begins with, or quickly breaks into, the drawbacks of the job. The job may even be described in totally negative terms. That is often done without giving a balanced view of the duties and expectations of the position.

Response: An initial negative description often means that the interviewer has had bad experiences hiring for the position. Your course is to empathize (not sympathize) with his or her bad experiences and make it known that you recognize the importance of (for example) reliability, especially in this particular type of job. (You will invariably find in these instances that what your interviewer has lacked in the past is someone with a serious understanding of value keys.) Illustrate your proficiency in that particular aspect of your profession with a short example from your work history. Finish your statements by asking the interviewer what some of the biggest problems to be handled in the job are. The questions demonstrate your understanding, and the interviewer's answers outline the areas from your background and skills to which you should draw attention.

☐ **Example Five:** The interviewer spends considerable time early in the interview describing "the type of people we are here at XYZ Corporation."

Response: Very simple. You have always wanted to work for a company with that atmosphere. It creates the type of work environment that is conducive to a person really giving his or her best efforts.

☐ **Example Six:** The interviewer asks closed-ended questions, ones that demand no more than a yes/no answer (e.g., "Do you pay attention to detail?"). Such questions are hardly adequate to establish your skills, yet you must handle them effectively to secure the job offer.

Response: A yes/no answer to a closed-ended question will not get you that offer. The trick is to treat each closed-ended question as if the interviewer has added, "Please give me a brief yet thorough answer." Closed-ended questions also are often mingled with statements followed by pauses. In those instances, agree with the statement in a way that demonstrates both a grasp of your job and the interviewer's statement. For example: "That's an excellent point, Mr. Smith. I couldn't agree more that the attention to detail you describe naturally affects cost containment. My track record in this area is . . ."

☐ **Example Seven:** The interviewer asks a continuing stream of negative questions (as described in Chapter 15, "The Stress Interview").

Response: Use the techniques and answers described earlier. Give your answers with a smile and do not take the questions as personal insults; they are not intended that way. The more stressful the situations the job is likely to place you in, the greater the likelihood of your having to field negative questions. The interviewer wants to know if you can take the heat.

☐ **Example Eight:** The interviewer has difficulty looking at you while speaking.

Response: The interviewer is someone who finds it uncomfortable being in the spotlight. Try to help him or her to be a good audience. Ask specific questions about the job responsibilities and offer your skills in turn.

☐ ☐ ☐

Often a hiring manager will arrange for you to meet with two or three other people. Frequently, the other interviewers have been neither trained in appropriate interviewing skills nor told the details of the job for which you are interviewing. So you will take additional copies of your executive briefing with you to the interview to aid them in focusing on the appropriate job functions.

When you understand how to recognize and respond to these different types of interviewer, you will leave your interview having made a favorable first impression. No one forgets first impressions.

15.
The Stress Interview

For all intents and purposes, every interview is a stress interview: The interviewer's negative and trick questions can act as the catalyst for your own fear. And the only way to combat that fear is to be prepared, to know what the interviewer is trying to do, to anticipate the various tacks he or she will take. Only preparedness will keep you cool and collected. Whenever you are ill-prepared for an interview, no one will be able to put more pressure on you than yourself. Remember: A stress interview is just a regular interview with the volume turned all the way up—the music's the same, just louder.

You've heard the horror stories. An interviewer demands of a hapless applicant, "Sell me this pen," or asks, "How would you improve the design of a teddy bear?" Or the candidate is faced with a battery of interviewers, all demanding rapid-fire answers to questions like, "You're giving a dinner party. Which ten famous people would you invite and why?" When the interviewee offers evidence of foot-in-mouth disease by asking, "Living or dead?" he receives his just desserts in reply: "Ten of each."

Such awful-sounding questions are thrown in to test your poise, to see how you react under pressure, and to plumb the depths of your confidence. Many people ruin their chances by reacting to them as personal insults rather than the challenge and opportunity to shine that they really represent.

Previously restricted to the executive suite for the selection of high-powered executives, stress interviews are now established throughout the professional world. And they can come complete with all the intimidating and treacherous tricks your worst nightmare can devise. Yet your good performance at a stress interview can mean the difference between life in the corporate fast lane and a stalled career. The interviewers in a stress interview are invariably experienced and well-organized, with tightly structured procedures and advanced interviewing techniques. The questions and tension they generate have the cumulative effect of throwing you off balance and revealing the "real" you—rather than someone who can respond with last night's rehearsed answers to six or seven stock questions.

Stress questions can be turned to your advantage or merely avoided by your nifty footwork. Whichever, you will be among a select few who understand this line of questioning. As always, remember with the questions in this chapter to build a personalized answer that reflects your experience and profession. Practice them aloud—by doing that, your responses to these interview gambits will become part of you, and that enhancement of your mental attitude will positively affect your confidence during an interview. You might even consider making a tape of tough questions, spacing then at intervals of 30 seconds to two minutes. You can then play the tape back and answer the questions in real time.

As we will see in this chapter, reflexive questions can prove especially useful when the heat is on. Stress questions are designed to sort out the clutch players from those who slow down under pressure. Used with discretion, the reflexives (". . . don't you think?") will demonstrate to the interviewer that you are able to function well under pressure. At the same time, of course, you put the ball back in the interviewer's court.

One common stress interview technique is to set you up for a fall: A pleasant conversation, one or a series of seemingly innocuous questions to relax your guard, then a dazzling series of jabs and body blows that leave you gibbering. For instance, an interviewer might lull you into a false sense of security by asking some relatively stressless questions: "What was your initial starting salary at your last job?" then, "What is your salary now?" then, "Do you receive bonuses?" etc. To put you on the ropes, he or she then completely surprises you with, "Tell me what sort of troubles you have living within your means," or "Why aren't you earning more at your age?" Such interviewers are using stress in an intelligent fashion, to simulate the unexpected and sometimes tense events of everyday business life. Seeing how you handle simulated pressure gives a fair indication of how you will react to the real thing.

The sophisticated interviewer talks very little, perhaps only 20 percent of the time, and that time is spent asking questions. Few comments, and no editorializing on your answers, means that you get no hint, verbal or otherwise, about your performance.

The questions are planned, targeted, sequenced, and layered. The interviewer covers one subject thoroughly before moving on. Let's take the simple example of "Can you work under pressure?" As a reader of *Knock 'em Dead*, you will know to answer that question with an example, and thereby deflect the main thrust of the stress technique. The interviewer will be prepared for a simple yes/no answer; what follows will keep the unprepared applicant reeling.

☐ *"Can you work under pressure?"* A simple, closed-ended question that requires just a yes/no answer, but you don't get off so easy.

☐ *"Good, I'd be interested to hear about a time when you experienced pressure on your job."* An open-ended request to tell a story about a pressure situation. After this, you will be subjected to the layering technique—six layers in the following instance. Imagine how tangled you could get without preparation.

☐ *"Why do you think this situation arose?"*

☐ *"When exactly did it happen?"* Watch out! Your story of saving thousands from the burning skyscraper may well be checked with your references.

☐ *"What in hindsight were you most dissatisfied with about your performance?"* Here we go. You're trying to show how well you perform under pressure, then suddenly you're telling tales against yourself.

☐ *"How do you feel others involved could have acted more responsibly?"* An open invitation to criticize peers and superiors, which you should diplomatically decline.

☐ *"Who holds the responsibility for the situation?"* Another invitation to point the finger of blame.

☐ *"Where in the chain of command could steps be taken to avoid that sort of thing happening again?"*

You have just been through an old reporters' technique of asking why, when, who, what, how, and where. That technique can be applied to any question you are asked and is frequently used to probe those success stories that sound just too good to be true. You'll find them suddenly tagged on to the simple closed-ended questions, as well as to the open-ended ones, starting, "Share with me," "Tell me about a time when," or, "I'm interested in finding out about," and requesting specific examples from your work history.

After you've survived that barrage, a friendly tone will conceal another zinger: "What did you learn from the experience?" It's a question that is geared to probing your judgment and emotional maturity. Your answer will be to emphasize whichever of the key personality traits your story was illustrating.

When the interviewer feels you were on the edge of revealing something unusual in an answer, you may well encounter "mirror statements." Here, the last key phrase of your answer will be repeated or paraphrased, and followed by a steady gaze and silence: "So, you learned that organization is the key to management." The idea is that the quiet and expectant look will work together to keep you talking. It can give you a most disconcerting feeling to find yourself rambling on without quite knowing why. The trick to that is knowing when to stop. When the interviewer gives you the expectant look, expand your answer (you have to), but by no more than a couple of sentences. Otherwise, you will get that creepy feeling that you're digging yourself into a hole.

There will be times when you face more than one interviewer at a time. When it happens, remember the story of one woman attorney who had five law partners all asking questions at the same time—as the poor interviewee got halfway through one answer, another question would be shot at her. Pausing for breath, she smiled and said, "Hold your horses, ladies and gentlemen. These are all excellent questions, and given time, I'll answer them all. Now who's next?" In so doing, she showed the interviewers exactly what they wanted to see and what, incidentally, is behind every stress interview and every negatively phrased question—finding the presence of poise and calm under fire, combined with a refusal to be intimidated.

You never know when a stress interview will raise its ugly head. Often it can be that rubber-stamp meeting with the senior V.P. at the end of a series of grueling meetings. That is not surprising: While other interviewers are concerned with determining whether you are able, willing, and manageable for the job in question, the senior executive who eventually throws you for a loop is the one who is probing you for potential promotability.

The most intimidating stress interviews are recognizable before the interviewer speaks: no eye contact, no greeting, either silence or a noncommittal grunt, no small talk. You may also recognize such an interviewer by his general air of boredom, disinterest, or thinly veiled aggression. The first words you hear could well be, "O.K., so go ahead. I don't have all day." In these situations, forewarned is forearmed, so here are some of the questions you can expect to follow such openings.

"What is your greatest weakness?"

This is a direct invitation to put your head in a noose. Decline the invitation.

If there is a minor part of the job at hand where you lack knowledge—but knowledge you will obviously pick up quickly—use that. For instance: "I haven't worked with this type of spreadsheet program before, but given my experience with six other types, I don't think it should take me more than a couple of days to pick it up." Here you remove the emphasis from weakness and put it onto a developmental problem that is easily overcome. Be careful, however: This very effective ploy must be used with discretion.

Another good option is to give a generalized answer that takes advantage of value keys. Design the answer so that your weakness is ultimately a positive characteristic. For example: "I enjoy my work and always give each project my best shot. So when sometimes I don't feel others are pulling their weight, I find it a little frustrating. I am aware of that weakness, and in those situations I try to overcome it with a positive attitude that I hope will catch on."

Also consider the technique of putting it in the past. Here you take a weakness from way back when, and show how you overcame it. It answers the question but ends on a positive note. An illustration: "When I first got into this field, I always had problems with my paperwork—you know, leaving an adequate paper trail. And to be honest, I let it slip once or twice. My manager sat me down and explained the potential troubles such behavior could cause. I really took it to heart, and I think you will find my paper trails some of the best around today. You only have to tell me something once." With that kind of answer, you also get the added bonus of showing that you accept and act on criticism.

Congratulations! You have just turned a bear of a question into an opportunity to sell yourself with your professional profile. In deciding on the particular answer you will give, remember that the interviewer isn't really concerned about your general weaknesses—none of us are saints outside of the interview room. He or she is simply concerned about any red flags that might signal your inability to perform the job or be manageable in the performance of your duties.

"With hindsight, how could you have improved your progress?"

Here's a question that demands, "Tell me your mistakes and weaknesses." If you can mention ways of improving your performance without damaging your candidacy, do so. The end of your answer should contain something like: "Other than that, I don't know what to add. I have always given it my best shot." Then shut up.

"What kind of decisions are most difficult for you?"

You are human, admit it, but be careful what you admit. If you have ever had to fire someone, you are in luck, because no one likes to do that. Emphasize that having reached a logical conclusion, you act. If you are not in management, tie your answer to key profiles: "It's not that I have difficulty making decisions—some just require more consideration than others. A small example might be vacation time. Now, everyone is entitled to it, but I don't believe you should leave your boss in a bind at short notice. I think very carefully at the beginning of the year when I'd like to take my vacation, and then think of alternate dates. I go to my supervisor, tell him what I hope to do, and see whether there is any conflict. I wouldn't want to be out of the office for the two weeks prior to a project deadline, for instance. So by carefully considering things far enough in advance, I don't procrastinate, and I make sure my plans jibe with my boss and the department for the year."

Here you take a trick question and use it to demonstrate your consideration, analytical abilities, and concern for the department—and for the company bottom line.

"Tell me about the problems you have living within your means."

This is a twister to catch you off guard. Your best defense is first of all to know that it exists, and secondly to give it short shrift. "I know few people who are satisfied with their current earnings. As a professional, I am continually striving to improve my skills and to improve my living standard. But my problems are no different from that of this company or any other—making sure all the bills get paid on time and recognizing that every month and year there are some things that are prudent to do and other expenses that are best deferred."

"What area of your skills/professional development do you want to improve at this time?"

Another tell-me-all-your-weaknesses question. You should try to avoid damaging your candidacy by tossing around careless admissions. One effective answer to this is to say, "Well, from what you told me about the job, I seem to have all the necessary skills and background. What I would really find exciting is the opportunity to work on a job where . . ." At this point, you replay the interviewer's hot buttons about the job. You emphasize that you really have all the job-related skills and also tell the interviewer what you find exciting about the job. It works admirably.

Another safe response is to reiterate one or two areas that combine personal strengths and the job's most crucial responsibilities, and finish with saying, "These areas are so important that I don't think anyone can be too good or should ever stop trying to polish skills."

"Your application shows you have been with one company a long time without any appreciable increase in rank or salary. Tell me about this."

Ugh. A toughie. To start with, you should analyze why this state of affairs does exist (assuming the interviewer's assessment is accurate). Then, when you have determined the cause, practice saying it out loud to yourself as you would say it during an actual interview. It may take a few tries. Chances are that no matter how valid your explanation really is, it will come off sounding a little tinny or vindictive without some polishing. Avoid the sour grapes syndrome at all costs.

Here are some tactics you can use. First of all, try to avoid putting your salary history on application forms. No one is going to deny you an interview for lack of a salary history if your skills match those the job requires. Of course, you should never put such trivia on your resume.

If the interviewer is intent, and asks you outright for this information, you'll find a great response on page 158, in the chapter on salary negotiations.

Now then. We address next the delicate matter of "hey-wait-a-minute-why-no-promotions?" This is one case where saying the wrong thing can get you in just as much trouble as failing to say the right thing. The interviewer has posed a truly negative inquiry; the more time either of you spend on it, the more time the interviewer gets to devote to concentrating on negative aspects of your candidacy. Make your answer short and sweet, then shut up. For instance, "My current employer is a stable company with a good working environment, but there's minimal growth there in my area—in fact, there hasn't been any promotion in my area since _____. Your question is the reason I am meeting here with you; I have the skills and ability to take on more responsibility and I'm looking for a place to do that."

"Are you willing to take calculated risks when necessary?"

First, qualify the question: "How do you define calculated risks? What sort of risks? Give me an example of a risk you have in mind; what are the stakes involved?" That will show you exactly the right analytical approach to evaluating a calculated risk, and while the interviewer is rattling on, you have bought time to come up with an answer. Whatever your answer, you will include, "Naturally, I would never take any risk that would in any way jeopardize the safety or reputation of my company or colleagues. In fact, I don't think any employer would appreciate an employee at any level taking risks of any nature without first having a thorough briefing and chance to give input."

"See this pen I'm holding? Sell it to me."

Not a request, as you might think, that would be asked only of a salesperson. In today's business world, everyone is required to sell—sometimes products, but more often ideas, approaches, and concepts. As such, you are being tested to see whether you understand the basic concepts of features-and-benefits selling, how quickly you think on your feet, and how effective your verbal communication is. For example, the interviewer holds up a broad-tip yellow highlighter. You say calmly, "Let me tell you about the special features of this product. First of all, it's a highlighter that will emphasize important points in reports or articles, and that will save you time in recalling the important features. The casing is wide enough to enable you to use it comfortably at your desk or on a flip chart. It has a flat base you can stand it up on. At one dollar, it is disposable—and affordable enough for you to have a handful for your desk, briefcase, car, and at home. And the bright yellow color means you'll never lose it."

Then close with a smile and a question of your own that will bring a smile to your interviewer's face: "How many gross shall we deliver?"

"How will you be able to cope with a change in environment after (e.g.) five years with your current company?"

Another chance to take an implied negative and turn it into a positive. "That's one of the reasons I want to make a change. After five years with my current employer, I felt I was about to get stale. Everyone needs a change of scene once in a while. It's just time for me to make some new friends, face some new challenges, and experience some new approaches; hopefully, I'll have the chance to contribute from my experience."

"Why aren't you earning more at your age?"

Accept this as a compliment to your skills and accomplishments. "I have always felt that solid experience would stand me in good stead in the long run and that earnings would come in due course. Also, I am not the type of person to change jobs just for the money. At this point, I have a solid background that is worth something to a company." Now, to avoid the interviewer putting you on the spot again, finish with a question: "How much should I be earning now?" The figure could be your offer.

"What is the worst thing you have heard about our company?"

If you have heard anything truly bad about the outfit, you shouldn't be there in the first place, so it is safe to assume you haven't. Regardless, the question can come as something of a shock. As with all stress questions, your poise under stress is vital: If you can carry off a halfway decent answer as well, you are a winner. The best response to this question is simple. Just say with a smile: "You're a tough company to get into because your interviews and interviewers are so rigorous." It's true, it's flattering, and it shows that you are not intimidated.

"How would you define your profession?"

With questions that solicit your understanding of a topic, no matter how good your answer, you can expect to be interrupted in mid-reply with "That has nothing to do with it," or, "Whoever put that idea into your head?" While your response is a judgment call, 999 times out of a thousand these comments are not meant to be taken as serious criticisms. Rather, they are tests to see how well you would be able to defend your position in a no-holds-barred conversation with the chairman of the board who says exactly what he or she thinks at all times. So go ahead and defend yourself, without taking or showing offense.

Your first response will be to gain time and get the interviewer talking. "Why do you say that?" you ask, answering a question with a question. And turning the tables on your aggressor displays your poise, calm, and analytical skills better than any other response.

"Why should I hire an outsider when I could fill the job with someone inside the company?"

The question isn't as stupid as it sounds. Obviously, the interviewer has examined existing employees with an eye toward their promotion or re-assignment. Just as obviously, the job cannot be filled from within the company. If it could be, it would be, and for two very good reasons: It is cheaper for the company to promote from within, and it is good for employee morale.

Hiding behind this intimidating question is actually a pleasant invitation: "Tell me why I should hire you." Your answer follows two steps. The first is a simple recitation of your skills and personality profile strengths, tailored to the specific requirements of the job.

For the second step, realize first that whenever a manager is filling a position, he or she is looking not only for someone who can do the job, but also for someone who can benefit the department in a larger sense. No department is as good as it could be each has weaknesses that need strengthening. So in the second part of your answer, include a question of your own: "Those are my general attributes. However, if no one is promotable from inside the company, that means you are looking to add strength to your team in a special way. In what ways do you hope the final candidate will be able to benefit your department?" The answer to this is your cue to sell your applicable qualities.

"Have you ever had any financial difficulties?"

The potential employer wants to know whether you can control not only your own finances, but finances in general. If you are in the insurance field, for example—claims, accounting, supervision, management—you can expect to hear this one. The question, though, is not restricted to insurance: Anyone, especially the person who handles money in day-to-day business, is fair game.

Remember that for someone to check your credit history, he or she must have your written consent. That is required under the 1972 Fair Credit and Reporting Act. When you fill out an application form, sign it, and date it, invariably somewhere on the form is a release permitting the employer to check your credit history. If you have already filled out the form, you might not hear the question, but your creditors might. I should note here that the reader who asked me about this question also described how she'd handled it during the interview: by describing her past problems with bankruptcy in every detail. However, in trying to be open and honest, she had actually done herself a disservice.

The interviewer does not want to hear sob-stories. Concentrate on the information that will damage your candidacy least and enhance it most. You might find it appropriate to bring the matter up yourself if you work in an area where your credit history is likely to be checked. If you choose to wait until the interviewer brings it up, you might say (if you had to file for bankruptcy, for instance), "I should tell you that some years ago, for reasons beyond my control, I was forced into personal bankruptcy. That has been behind me for some time. Today, I have a sound credit rating and no debts. Bankruptcy is not something I'm proud of, but I did learn from the experience, and I feel it has made me a more proficient account supervisor." The answer concentrates on today, not past history.

"How do you handle rejection?"

This question is common if you are applying for a job in sales, including face-to-face sales, telemarketing, public relations, and customer service. If you are after a job in one of these areas and you really don't like the heavy doses of rejection that are any salesperson's lot, consider a new field. The anguish you will experience will not lead to a successful career or a happy life.

With that in mind, let's look behind the question. The interviewer simply wants to know whether you take rejection as rejection of yourself or whether you simply accept it as a temporary rejection of a service or product. Here is a sample answer that you can tailor to your particular needs and background: "I accept rejection as an integral part of the sales process. If everyone said yes to a product, there would be no need for the sales function. As it is, I see every rejection as bringing me closer to the customer who will say yes." Then, if you are encouraged to go on: "I regard rejection as simply a fact of life, that the customer has no need for the product today. I can go on to my next call with the conviction that I am a little closer to my next sale."

"Why were you out of work for so long?"

You must have a sound explanation for any and all gaps in your employment history. If not, you are unlikely to receive a job offer. Emphasize that you were not just looking for another paycheck—you were looking for a company with which to settle and to which to make a long-term contribution.

"I made a decision that I enjoy my work too much just to accept another paycheck. So I determined that the next job I took would be one where I could settle down and do my best to make a solid contribution. From everything I have heard about this company, you are a group that expects people to pull their weight, because you've got a real job to do. I like that, and I would like to be part of the team. What have I got to do to get the job?"

You answer the question, compliment the interviewer, and shift the emphasis from you being unemployed to how you can get the job offer.

"Why have you changed jobs so frequently?"

If you have jumped around, blame it on youth (even the interviewer was young once). Now you realize what a mistake your job-hopping was, and with your added domestic responsibilities you are now much more settled. Or you may wish to impress on the interviewer that your job-hopping was never as a result of poor performance, and that you grew professionally as a result of each job change.

You could reply: "My first job was a very long commute. I soon realized that, but I knew it would give me good experience in a very competitive field. Subsequently, I found a job much closer to home where the commute was only an hour each way. I was very happy at my second job. However, I got an opportunity to really broaden my experience base with a new company that was starting up. With the wisdom of hindsight, I realize that was a mistake; it took me six months to realize I couldn't make a contribution there. I've been with my current company a reasonable length of time. So I have broad experience in different environments. I didn't just job-hop, I have been following a path to gain broad experience. So you see, I have more experience than the average person of my years, and a desire to settle down and make it pay off for me and my employer."

Or you can say: "Now I want to settle down and make all my diverse background pay off in my contributions to my new employer. I have a strong desire to contribute and am looking for an employer that will keep me challenged, I think this might be the company to do that. Am I right?"

"Tell me about a time when you put your foot in your mouth."

Answer this question with caution. The interviewer is examining your ability and willingness to interact pleasantly with others. The question is tricky because it asks you to show yourself in a poor light. Your answer will downplay the negative impact of your action and will end with positive information about your candidacy. The best thing to do is to start with an example outside of the workplace, and show how the experience improved your performance at work.

"About five years ago, I let the cat out of the bag about a surprise birthday party for a friend, a terrific *faux pas*. It was a mortifying experience, and I promised myself not to let anything like that happen again." Then, after this fairly innocuous statement, you can talk about communications in the workplace. "As far as work is concerned, I always regard employer/employee communications on any matter as confidential unless expressly stated otherwise. So, putting my foot in my mouth doesn't happen to me at work."

"Why do you want to leave your current job?" or, *"Why did you leave your last job?"*

This is a common trick question. You should have an acceptable reason for leaving every job you have held, but if you don't, pick one of the six acceptable reasons from the employment industry formula, the acronym for which is CLAMPS:

- **Challenge:** You weren't able to grow professionally in that position.

- **Location:** The commute was unreasonably long.

- **Advancement:** There was nowhere for you to go. You had the talent, but there were too many people ahead of you.

- **Money:** You were underpaid for your skills and contribution.

- **Pride or prestige:** You wanted to be with a better company.

- **Security:** The company was not stable.

For example: "My last company was a family-owned affair. I had gone as far as I was able. It just seemed time for me to join a more prestigious company and accept greater challenges."

"What interests you least about this job?"

This question is potentially explosive, but easily defused. Regardless of your occupation, there is at least one repetitive, mindless duty that everyone groans about and that goes with the territory. Use that as your example in a statement of this nature: "Filing is probably the least demanding part of the job. However, it is important to the overall success of my department, so I try to do it with a smile." This shows that you understand that it is necessary to take the rough with the smooth in any job.

"What was there about your last company that you didn't particularly like or agree with?"

You are being checked out as a potential fly in the ointment. If you have to answer, it might be the way the company policies and/or directives were sometimes consciously misunderstood by some employees who disregard the bottom line—the profitability of the corporation.

Or: "You know how it is sometimes with a big company. People lose awareness of the cost of things. There never seemed to be much concern about economy or efficiency. Everyone wanted his or her year-end bonus, but only worried about it in December. The rest of the year, nobody gave a hoot. I think that's the kind of thing we could be aware of most every day, don't you agree?"

Or: "I didn't like the way some people gave lip-service to 'the customer comes first,' but really didn't go out of their way to keep the customer satisfied. I don't think it was a fault of management, just a general malaise that seemed to affect a lot of people."

"What do you feel is a satisfactory attendance record?"

There are two answers to this question—one if you are in management, one if you are not. As a manager: "I believe attendance is a matter of management, motivation, and psychology. Letting the employees know you expect their best efforts and won't accept half-baked excuses is one thing. The other is to keep your employees motivated by a congenial work environment and the challenge to stretch themselves. Giving people pride in their work and letting them know you respect them as individuals have a lot to do with it, too."

If you are not in management, the answer is even easier: "I've never really considered it. I work for a living, I enjoy my job, and I'm rarely sick."

"What is your general impression of your last company?"

Always answer positively. Keep your real feelings to yourself, whatever they might be. There is a strong belief among the management fraternity that people who complain about past employers will cause problems for their new ones. Your answer is, "Very good" or, "Excellent." Then smile and wait for the next question.

"What are some of the problems you encounter in doing your job, and what do you do about them?"

Note well the old saying, "A poor workman blames his tools." Your awareness that careless mistakes cost the company good money means you are always on the lookout for potential problems. Give an example of a problem you recognized and solved.

For example: "My job is fairly repetitive, so it's easy to overlook problems. Lots of people do. However, I always look for them; it helps keep me alert and motivated, so I do a better job. To give you an example, we make computer-memory disks. Each one has to be machined by hand, and once completed, the slightest abrasion will turn one into a reject. I have a steady staff and little turnover, and everyone wears cotton gloves to handle the disks. Yet about six months ago, the reject rate suddenly went through the roof. Is that the kind of problem you mean? Well, the cause was one that could have gone unnoticed for ages. Jill, the section head who inspects all the disks, had lost a lot of weight, her diamond engagement ring slipped around her finger, and it was scratching the disks as she passed them and stacked them to be shipped. Our main client was giving us a big problem over it, so my looking for problems and paying attention to detail really paid off."

The interviewer was trying to get you to reveal weak points; you avoided the trap.

"What are some of the things you find difficult to do? Why do you feel that way?"

This is a variation on a couple of earlier questions. Remember, anything that goes against the best interests of your employer is difficult to do. If you are pressed for a job function you find difficult, answer in the past tense; that way, you show that you recognize the difficulty, but that you obviously handle it well.

"That's a tough question. There are so many things that are difficult to learn in our business if you want to do the job right. I used to have 40 clients to sell to every month, and I was so busy touching bases with all of them, I never got a chance to sell to any of them. So I graded them into three groups. I call on the top 20 percent with whom I did business every three weeks. The next group were those I sold to occasionally. I called on them once a month, but with a difference—each month, I marked 10 of them to spend time with and really get to know. I still have difficulty reaching all 40 of my clients in a month, but my sales have tripled and are still climbing."

"Jobs have plusses and minuses. What were some of the minuses on your last job?"

A variation on the question, "What interests you least about this job?" which was handled earlier. Use the same type of answer. For example, "Like any salesperson, I enjoy selling, not doing the paperwork. But as I cannot expect the customer to get the goods, and me my commission, without following through on this task, I grin and bear it. Besides, if I don't do the paperwork, that holds up other people in the company."

If you are not in sales, use the salesforce as a scapegoat. "In accounts receivable, it's my job to get the money in to make payroll and good things like that. Half the time, the goods get shipped before I get the paperwork because sales says, 'It's a rush order.' That's a real minus to me. It was so bad at my last company, we tried a new approach. We met with sales and explained our problem. The result was that incremental commissions were based on cash in, not on bill date. They saw the connection, and things are much better now."

"What kind of people do you like to work with?"

This is the easy part of a tricky three-part question. Obviously, you like to work with people who have pride, honesty, integrity, and dedication to their work. Now—

"What kind of people do you find it difficult to work with?"

The second part of the same question. You could say: "People who don't follow procedures, or slackers—the occasional rotten apples who don't really care about the quality of their work. They're long on complaints, but short on solutions." Which brings us to the third part of the question:

"How have you successfully worked with this difficult type of person?"

This is the most difficult part to answer. You might reply: "I stick to my guns, keep enthusiastic, and hope some of it will rub off. I had a big problem with one guy—all he did was complain and always in my area. Eventually, I told him how I felt. I said if I were a millionaire, I'd have all the answers and wouldn't have to work, but as it was, I wasn't, and had to work for a living. I told him that I really enjoyed his company, but I didn't want to hear it any more. Every time I saw him after that, I presented him with a work problem and asked his advice. In other words I challenged him to come up with positives, not negatives."

You can go on that sometimes you've noticed that such people simply lack enthusiasm and confidence, and that energetic and cheerful co-workers can often change that. If the interviewer follows up with an inquiry about what you would do if no amount of good effort on your part solved the problem, respond, "I would maintain cordial relations, but not go out of my way to seek more than a business-like acquaintance. Life is too short to be demotivated by people who always think their cup is half empty."

"How did you get your last job?"

The interviewer is looking for initiative. If you can, show it. At the least, show determination.

"I was actually turned down for my last job as having too little experience. I asked the manager to give me a trial before she offered it to anyone else. I went in and asked for a list of companies they'd never sold to, picked up the phone, and in that hour I arranged two appointments. How did I get the job? In a word, determination!"

"How would you evaluate me as an interviewer?"

The question is dangerous, maybe more so than the one asking you to criticize your boss. Whatever you do, of course, don't tell the truth if you think the interviewer is an unconscious incompetent. It may be true, but it won't get you a job offer. This is an instance where honesty is not the best policy. It is best to say, "This is one of the toughest interviews I have ever been through, and I don't relish the prospect of going through another. Yet I do realize what you are trying to achieve." Then go on to explain that you understand the interviewer wants to know whether you can think on your feet, that there is pressure on the job, and that he or she is trying to simulate some of that real-life pressure in the interview. You may choose to finish the answer with a question of your own: "How do you think I fit the profile of the person you need?"

"I'm not sure you're suitable for the job."

Don't worry about the tone of the question—the interviewer's "I'm not sure" really means, "I'd like to hire you, so here's a wide open opportunity to sell me." He or she is probing three areas from your personal profile: your confidence, determination, and listening profiles. Remain calm and put the ball straight back into the interviewer's court: "Why do you say that?" You need both the information and time to think up an appropriate reply, but it is important to show that you are not intimidated. Work out a program of action for this question; even if the interviewer's point regarding your skills is valid, come back with value keys and alternate compatible skills. You counter with other skills that show your competence and learning ability, and use them to show you can pick up the new skills quickly. Tie the two together and demonstrate that with your other attributes you can bring many plusses to the job. Finish your answer with a reflexive question that encourages a "yes" answer.

"I admit my programming skills in that language are a little light. However, all languages have similarities, and my experience demonstrates that with a competence in four other languages, getting up to speed with this one will take only a short while. Plus, I can bring a depth of other experience to the job." Then, after you itemize your experience: "Wouldn't you agree?"

If the reason for the question is not a lack of technical skills, it must be a question about one of your key profile areas. Perhaps the interviewer will say, "You haven't convinced me of your determination." This is an invitation to sell yourself, so tell a story that demonstrates determination.

For example: "It's interesting you should say that. My present boss is convinced of my determination. About a year ago we were having some problems with a union organization in the plant. Management's problem was our 50 percent Spanish monolingual production workforce. Despite the fact that our people had the best working conditions and benefits in the area, they were strongly pro-union. If they were successful, we would be the first unionized division in the company. No one in management spoke Spanish, so I took a crash Berlitz course—two hours at home every night for five weeks. I got one of the maintenance crew to help me with my grammar and diction. Then a number of other production workers started saying simple things to me in Spanish and helping me with the answers. I opened the first meeting with the workforce to discuss the problems. My 'Buenos dias. Me llamo Brandon,' got a few cheers. We had demonstrated that we cared enough to try to communicate. Our division never did unionize, and my determination to take the extra step paid off and allowed my superiors to negotiate from a position of caring and strength. That led to English lessons for the Spanish-speaking, and Spanish classes for the English-speaking. We are now a bilingual company, and I think that shows we care. Wouldn't you agree my work in that instance shows determination?"

"Wouldn't you feel better off in another firm?"

Relax, things aren't as bad as you might assume. This question is usually asked if you are really doing quite well, or if the job involves a certain amount of stress. A lawyer, for example, might well be expected to face this one. The trick is not to be intimidated. Your first step is to qualify the question: Relax, take a breath, sit back, smile, and say, "You surprise me. Why do you say that?" The interviewer must then talk, giving you precious time to collect your wits and come back with a rebuttal.

Then answer "no" and explain why. All the interviewer wants to see is how much you know about the company and how determined you are to join its ranks. Your earlier research and knowledge of personal profile keys (determination) will pay off again. Overcome the objection with an example, and show how that will help you contribute to the company; end with a question of your own. In this instance, the question has a twofold purpose: one, to identify a critical area to sell yourself; and two, to encourage the interviewer to consider an image of you working at the company.

You could reply: "Not at all. My whole experience has been with small companies. I am good at my job and in time could become a big fish in a little pond. But that is not what I want. This corporation is a leader in its business. You have a strong reputation for encouraging skills-development in your employees. This is the type of environment I want to work in. Now, coming from a small company, I have done a little bit of everything. That means that no matter what you throw at me, I will learn it quickly. For example, what would be the first project I would be involved with?"

And you end with a question of your own that gets the interviewer focusing on those immediate problems. You can then explain how your background and experience can help.

"What would you say if I told you your presentation this afternoon was lousy?"

"If" is the key here, with the accusation only there for the terminally neurotic. The question is designed to see how you react to criticism, and so tests manageability. No company can afford the thin-skinned today. You will come back and answer the question with a question of your own.

An appropriate response would be: "First of all, I would ask which aspects of my presentation were lousy. My next step would be to find out where you felt the problem was. If there'd been miscommunication, I'd clear it up. If the problem were elsewhere, I would seek your advice and be sure that the problem was not recurrent." This would show that when it is a manager's duty to criticize performance, you are an employee who will respond in a businesslike and emotionally mature manner.

The Illegal Question

Of course, one of the most stressful—and negative—questions is the illegal one, a question that delves into your private life or personal background. Such a question will make you uncomfortable if it is blatant, and could also make you angry.

Your aim, however, is to overcome the discomfort and to avoid anger: You want to get the job offer, and any self-righteousness or defensive reaction on your part will ensure that you *don't* get it. You may feel angry enough to get up and walk out, or say things like, "These are unfair practices; you'll hear from my lawyer in the morning." But the result will be that you won't get the offer, and therefore won't have the leverage you need. Remember, no one is saying you can't refuse the job once it's offered to you.

But what is an illegal question? Title VII is a federal law that forbids employers from discriminating against any person on the basis of sex, age, race, national origin, or religion. In addition, many states have laws that protect people who fall into other categories, such as the physically challenged. Here are some general guidelines interviewers must follow.

☐ An interviewer may not ask about your religion, church, synagogue, parish, the religious holidays you observe, or your political beliefs or affiliations. He or she may not ask, for instance, "Does your religion allow you to work on Saturdays?" *But*, the interviewer may ask something like, "This job requires work on Saturdays. Is that a problem?"

□ An interviewer may not ask about your ancestry, national origin, or parentage; in addition, you cannot be asked about the naturalization status of your parents, spouse, or children. The interviewer cannot ask about your birthplace. *But,* the interviewer may ask (and probably will, considering the current immigration laws) whether you are a U.S. citizen or a resident alien with the right to work in the U.S.

□ An interviewer may not ask about your native language, the language you speak at home, or how you acquired the ability to read, write, or speak a foreign language. *But,* he or she may ask about the languages in which you are fluent, if knowledge of those languages is pertinent to the job.

□ An interviewer may not ask about your age, your date of birth, or the ages of your children. *But,* he or she may ask you whether you are over 18 years old.

□ An interviewer may not ask about maiden names or whether you have changed your name; your marital status, number of children or dependents, or your spouse's occupation; or whether (if you are a woman) you wish to be addressed as Miss, Mrs., or Ms. *But,* the interviewer may ask about *how* you like to be addressed (a common courtesy) and whether you have ever worked for the company before under a different name. (If you have worked for this company or other companies under a different name, you may want to mention that, in light of the fact that this prospective manager may check your references and additional background information.)

As you consider a question that seems to verge on illegality, you should take into account that the interviewer may be asking it innocently, and may be unaware of the laws on the matter. Your best bet is to be polite and straightforward, as you would in any other social situation. You also want to move the conversation to an examination of your skills and abilities, not your status. Here are some illegal questions—and some possible responses. Remember, your objective is to get job offers; if you later decide that this company is not for you, you are under no obligation to accept the position.

"What religion do you practice?"

If you do practice, you can say, "I attend my church/synagogue/mosque regularly, but I make it my practice not to involve my personal beliefs in my work. The work for the company and my career are too important for that."

If you do not practice a religion, you may want to say something like, "I have a set of personal beliefs that are important to me, but I do not attend any organized services. And I do not mix those beliefs with my work, if that's what you mean."

"How old are you?"

Old-age discrimination is still prevalent, but with older people joining the workforce every day and the increasing need for experienced workers, you will hear this question less and less. Answer the question in terms of your experience. For example: "I'm in my fifties and have more than 25 years of experience in this field." Then list your skills as they apply to the job.

"Are you married?"

If you are, the company is concerned with the impact your family duties and future plans will have on your tenure there. Your answer could be, "Yes, I am. Of course, I make a separation between my work life and my family life that allows me to give my all to a job. I have no problem with travel or late hours—those things are part of this line of work. I'm sure my references will confirm this for you."

"Do you plan to have children?"

This isn't any of the interviewer's business, but he or she wants to know whether you will leave the company early to raise a family. You can answer "no," of course. If you answer 'yes,' you might add, "But those plans are for the future, and they depend on the success of my career. Certainly, I want to do the best, most complete job for this company I can. I consider that my skills are right for the job and that I can make a long-range contribution. I certainly have no plans to leave the company just as I begin to make meaningful contributions."

If the questions become too pointed, you may want to ask—innocently—"Could you explain the relevance of that issue to the position? I'm trying to get a handle on it." That response, however, can seem confrontational; you should only use it if you are *extremely* uncomfortable, or are quite certain you can get away with it. Sometimes, the interviewer will drop the line of questioning.

Illegal questions tend to arise, not out of brazen insensitivity, but rather out of an interest in you. The employer is familiar with your skills and background, feels you can do the job, and wants to get to know you as a person. Outright discrimination these days is really quite rare. With illegal questions, your response must be positive—that's the only way you're going to get the job offer, and getting a job offer allows you to leverage other jobs. You don't have to work for a discriminatory company, but you can certainly use the firm to get to something better.

□□□

Interviewers may pull all kinds of tricks on you, but you will come through with flying colors once you realize that they're trying to discover something extremely simple—whether or not you can take the heat. After all, those interviewers are only trying to sort out the good corporate warriors from the walking wounded. If you are asked and successfully handle these trick and negatively phrased questions, the interviewer will end up looking at you favorably. Stay calm, give as good as you get, and take it all in good part. Remember that no one can intimidate you without your permission.

16.
Strange Venues

Why are some interviews conducted in strange places? Are meetings in noisy, distracting hotel lobbies designed as a form of torture? What are the real reasons that an interviewer invites you to eat at a fancy restaurant?

For the most part, these tough-on-the-nerves situations happen because the interviewer is a busy person, fitting you into a busy schedule. Take the case of a woman I know. She had heard stories about tough interview situations but never expected to face one herself. It happened at a retail convention in Arizona, and she had been asked to meet for a final interview by the pool. The interviewer was there, taking a short break between meetings, in his bathing suit. And the first thing the interviewer did was suggest that my friend slip into something comfortable.

That scenario may not lurk in your future, but the chances are that you will face many tough interview situations in your career. They call for a clear head and a little gamesmanship to put you ahead of the competition. The interviewee at the pool used both. She removed her jacket, folded it over the arm of the chair and seated herself, saying pleasantly, "That's much better. Where shall we begin?"

It isn't easy to remain calm at such times. On top of interview nerves, you're worried about being overheard in a public place, or (worse) surprised by the appearance of your current boss. That last item isn't too far-fetched. It actually happened to a reader from San Francisco. He was being interviewed in the departure lounge at the airport when his boss walked through the arrivals door. Oops—he had asked for the day off "to go to the doctor."

Could he have avoided the situation? Certainly, if he had asked about privacy when the meeting was arranged. That would have reminded the interviewer of the need for discretion. The point is to do all you can in advance to make such a meeting as private as possible. Once that's done, you can ignore the rest of the world and concentrate on the interviewer's questions.

Hotel Lobbies and Other Strange Places

Strange interview situations provide other wonderful opportunities to embarrass yourself. You come to a hotel lobby in full corporate battle dress: coat, briefcase, perhaps an umbrella. You sit down to wait for the interviewer. "Aha," you think to yourself, opening your briefcase, "I'll show him my excellent work habits by delving into this computer printout."

That's not such a great idea. Have you ever tried rising with your lap covered with business papers, then juggling the briefcase from right hand to left to accommodate the ritual handshake? It's quite difficult. Besides, while you are sitting in nervous anticipation, pre-interview tension has no way of dissipating. Your mouth will become dry, and your "Good morning, I'm pleased to meet you" will come out sounding like the cat being strangled.

To avoid such catastrophes in places like hotel lobbies, first remove your coat on arrival. Then, instead of sitting, walk around a little while you wait. Even in a small lobby, a few steps back and forth will help you reduce tension to a manageable level. Keep your briefcase in your left hand at all times—it makes you look purposeful, and you won't trip over it when you meet the interviewer.

If, for any reason, you must sit down, make a conscious effort to breathe deeply and slowly. This will help control the adrenaline that makes you feel jumpy.

A strange setting can actually put you on equal footing with the interviewer. Neither of you is on home turf, so in many cases, the interviewer will feel just as awkward as you do. A little gamesmanship can turn the occasion to your advantage.

To gain the upper hand, get to the meeting site early to scout the territory. By knowing your surroundings, you will feel more relaxed. Early arrival also allows you to control the outcome of the meeting in other subtle ways. You will have time to stake out the most private spot in an otherwise public place. Corners are best. They tend to be quieter, and you can choose the seat that puts your back to the wall (in a practical sense, that is). In this position, you have a clear view of your surroundings and will feel more secure. The fear of being overheard will evaporate.

The situation is now somewhat in your favor. You know the locale, and the meeting place is as much yours as the interviewer's. You will have a clear view of your surroundings, and odds are that you will be more relaxed than the interviewer. When he or she arrives, say, "I arrived a little early to make sure we had some privacy. I think over here is the best spot." With that positive demonstration of your organizational abilities, you give yourself a head start over the competition.

The Meal Meeting

Breakfast, lunch, or dinner are the prime choices for interviewers who want to catch the seasoned professional off guard. In fact, the meal is arguably the toughest of all tough interview situations. The setting offers the interviewer the chance to see you in a nonoffice (and therefore more natural) setting, to observe your social graces, and to consider you as a whole person. Here, topics that would be impossible to address in the traditional office setting will naturally surface, often with virtually no effort on the part of the interviewer. The slightest slip in front of that wily old sea pirate opposite—thinly disguised in a Brooks Brothers suit—could get your candidacy deep-sixed *tout suite.*

Usually, you will not be invited to an "eating meeting" until you have already demonstrated that you are capable of doing the job. It's a good sign, actually: An invitation to a meal means that you are under strong consideration, and, by extension, intense scrutiny.

The meeting is often the final hurdle and could lead directly to the job offer—assuming, of course, that you properly handle the occasional surprises that arise. The interviewer's concern is not whether you can do the job, but whether you have the growth potential that will allow you to fill more senior slots as they become available.

But be careful. Many have fallen at the final hurdle in a close-run race. Being interviewed in front of others is bad enough; eating and drinking in front of them at the same time only makes it worse. If you knock over a glass or dribble spaghetti sauce down your chin, the interviewer will be so busy smirking that he or she won't hear what you have to say.

To be sure that the interviewer remains as attentive to the positive points of your candidacy as possible, let's discuss table manners.

Your social graces and general demeanor at the table can tell as much about you as your answer to a question. For instance, over-ordering food or drink can signal poor self-discipline. At the very least, it will call into question your judgment and maturity. High-handed behavior toward waiters and buspeople could reflect negatively on your ability to get along with subordinates and on your leadership skills. Those concerns are amplified when you return food or complain about the service, actions which, at the very least, find fault with the interviewer's choice of restaurant.

By the same token, you will want to observe how your potential employer behaves. After all, you are likely to become an employee, and the interviewer's behavior to servers in a restaurant can tell you a lot about what it will be like on the job.

☐ **Alcohol:** Soon after being seated, you will be offered a drink—if not by your host, then by the waiter. There are many reasons to avoid alcohol at interview meals. The most important reason is that alcohol fuzzes your mind, and research proves that stress increases the intoxicating effect of alcohol. So, if you order something to drink, try to stick with something nonalcoholic, such as a club soda or simply a glass of water. If pressed, order a white-wine spritzer, a sherry, or a light beer—it depends on the environment and what your host is drinking.

If you do have a drink, never have more than one. If there is a bottle of wine on the table, and the waiter offers you another glass, simply place your hand over the top of your glass. It is a polite way of signifying no.

You may be offered alcohol at the end of the meal. The rule still holds true—turn it down. You need your wits about you even if the interview seems to be drawing to a close. Some interviewers will try to use those moments, when your defenses are at their lowest, to throw in a couple of zingers.

☐ **Smoking:** Smoking is another big problem that is best handled by taking a simple approach. Don't do it unless encouraged. If both of you are smokers, and you are encouraged to smoke, follow a simple rule: Never smoke between courses, only at the end of a meal. Even most confirmed nicotine addicts, like the rest of the population, hate smoke while they are eating.

☐ **Utensils:** Keep all your cups and glasses at the top of your place setting and well away from you. Most glasses are knocked over at a cluttered table when one stretches for the condiments or gesticulates to make a point. Of course, your manners will prevent you from reaching rudely for the pepper-shaker.

When you are faced with an array of knives, forks, and spoons, it is always safe to start at the outside and work your way in as the courses come. Keep your elbows at your sides and don't slouch in the chair. When pausing between mouthfuls (which, if you are promoting yourself properly, should be frequently), rest your knife and fork on the plate this way.

The time to start eating, of course, is when the interviewer does; the time to stop is when he or she does. At the end of a course or the meal, rest your knife and fork together on the plate, at five o'clock.

Here are some other helpful hints:

- Never speak with your mouth full.

- To be on the safe side, eat the same thing, or close to it, as the interviewer. Of course, while this rule makes sense in theory, the fact is that you probably will be asked to order first, so ordering the same thing can become problematic. Solve the problem before you order by complimenting the restaurant during your small talk and then, when the menus arrive, asking, "What do think you will have today?"

- Do not change your order once it is made, and never send the food back.

- Be polite to your waiters, even when they spill soup in your lap.

- Don't order expensive food. Naturally, in our heart of hearts, we all like to eat well, especially on someone else's tab. But don't be tempted. When you come right down to it, you are there to talk and be seen at your best, not to eat.

- Eat what you know. Stay away from awkward, messy, or exotic foods (e.g., artichokes, long pasta, and escargot, respectively). Ignore finger foods, such as lobster or spare ribs. In fact, you should avoid eating with your fingers altogether, unless you are in a sandwich joint, in which case you should make a point of avoiding the leaky, over-stuffed menu items.

- Don't order salad. The dressing can often get messy. If a salad comes with the meal, request that the dressing be on the side. Then, before pouring it on, cut up the lettuce.

- Don't order anything with bones. Stick with filets; there are few simple, gracious ways to deal with any type of bone.

□ **Checks and Goodbyes:** I know an interviewer whose favorite test of composure is to have the waiter, by arrangement, put the bill on the interviewee's side of the table. She then chats on, waiting for something interesting to happen. If you ever find yourself in a similar situation, never pick up the check, however long it is left by your plate. When ready, your host will pick it up, because that's the simple protocol of the occasion. By the same token, you should never offer to share payment.

When parting company, always thank the host for his or her hospitality and the wonderful meal. Of course, you should be sure to leave on a positive note by asking good naturedly what you have to do to get the job.

Strange interview situations can arise at any time during the interview cycle, and in any public place. Wherever you are asked to go, keep your guard up. Your table manners, listening skills, and overall social graces are being judged. The question on the interviewer's mind is: Can you be trusted to represent the company graciously?

17.
Welcome to
the Real World

Of all the steps a recent graduate will take up the ladder of success over the years, none is more important or more difficult than getting a foot on the first rung. And the interviewing process designed for recent graduates is particularly rigorous, because management regards the hiring of entry-level professionals as one of its toughest jobs.

When a company hires experienced people, there is a track record to evaluate. With recent graduates, there is little or nothing. Often, the only solid things an interviewer has to go on are high-school, SAT, and/or college grades. That's not much on which to base a hiring decision—grades don't tell the interviewer whether you will fit in or make a reliable employee. Many recruiters liken the gamble of hiring recent graduates to laying down wines for the future: They know that some will develop into full-bodied, reliable vintages, but that others will be disappointments. So, recruiters have to find different ways to predict your potential accurately.

After relying, as best they can, on school performance to evaluate your ability, interviewers concentrate on questions that reveal how willing you are to learn and get the job done, and how manageable you are likely to be, both on average days and when the going gets rough.

Your goal is to stand out from all the other entry-level candidates as someone altogether different and better. For example, don't be like thousands of others who, in answer to questions about their greatest strength, reply lamely, "I'm good with people," or, "I like working with others." As you know by now, such answers do not separate you from the herd. In fact, they brand you as average. To stand out, a recent graduate must recount a past situation that illustrates how good he or she is with people, or one that demonstrates an ability to be a team player.

Fortunately, the key personality traits discussed throughout the book are just as helpful for getting your foot on the ladder as they are for aiding your climb to the top. They will guide you in choosing what aspects of your personality and background you should promote at the interview.

It isn't necessary to have snap answers ready for every question, because you never will. In fact, it is more important for you to pause after a question and collect your thoughts before answering: You must show that you think before you speak. That way, you will demonstrate your analytical abilities, which age feels youth has in short supply.

By the same token, occasionally asking for a question to be repeated is useful to gain time and is quite acceptable, as long as you don't do it with every question. And if a question stumps you, as sometimes happens, do not stutter incoherently. It is sometimes best to say simply, "I don't know." Or, you might say, "I'd like to come back to that later"–the odds are even that the interviewer will forget to ask again; if he or she doesn't, at least you've had some time to come up with an answer.

Knowing everything about a certain entry-level position is not necessary, because business feels it can teach you most things. But, as a vice president of Merrill Lynch once said, "You must bring to the table the ability to speak clearly." So, knowing what is behind those questions designed especially for recent graduates will give you the time to build informative and understandable answers.

"How did you get your summer jobs?"

All employers look favorably on recent graduates who have any work experience, no matter what it is. "It is far easier to get a fix on someone who has worked while at school," says Dan O'Brien, head of employment at Grumman Aerospace. "They manage their time better, are more realistic, and more mature. Any work experience gives us much more in common." So, as you make your answer, add that you learned that business is about making a profit, doing things more efficiently, adhering to procedures, and putting out whatever effort it takes to get the job done. In short, treat your summer jobs, no matter how humble, as any other business experience.

In this particular question, the interviewer is looking ideally for something that shows initiative, creativity, and flexibility. Here's an example: "In my town, summer jobs were hard to come by, but I applied to each local restaurant for a position waiting tables, called the manager at each one to arrange an interview, and finally landed a job at one of the most prestigious. I was assigned to the afternoon shift, but with my quick work, accurate billing, and ability to keep customers happy, they soon moved me to the evening shift. I worked there for three summers, and by the time I left, I was responsible for the training and management of the night-shift waiters, the allotment of tips, and the evening's final closing and accounting. All in all, my experience showed me the mechanics of a small business and of business in general."

"Which of the jobs you have held have you liked least?"

The interviewer is trying to trip you up. It is likely that your work experience contained a certain amount of repetition and drudgery, as all early jobs in the business world do. So beware of saying that you hated a particular job "because it was boring." Avoid the negative and say something along these lines: "All of my jobs had their good and bad points, but I've always found that if you want to learn, there's plenty to be picked up every day. Each experience was valuable." Then describe a seemingly boring job, but show how it taught you valuable lessons or helped you hone different aspects of your personality profile.

"What are your future vocational plans?"

This is a fancy way of asking, "Where do you want to be five years from now?" The trap all entry-level professionals make is to say, "In management," because they think that shows drive and ambition. It has become such a trite answer, though, that it immediately generates a string of questions that most recent graduates can't answer: What is the definition of management? What is a manager's prime responsibility? A manager in what area? Your safest answer identifies you with the profession you are trying to break into, and shows you have your feet on the ground. "My vocational plans are that I want to get ahead. To do that I must be able to channel my energies and expertise into those areas my industry and employer need. So given a couple of years I hope to have become a thorough professional with a clear understanding of the company, the industry, and where the biggest challenges, and therefore opportunities, lie. By that time, my goals for the future should be sharply defined." An answer like that will set you far apart from your contemporaries.

"What college did you attend, and why did you choose it?"

The college you attended isn't as important as your reasons for choosing it—the question is trying to examine your reasoning processes. Emphasize that it was your choice, and that you didn't go there as a result of your parents' desires or because generations of your family have always attended the Acme School of Welding. Focus on the practical. "I went to Greenbriar State—it was a choice based on practicality. I wanted a school that would give me a good education and prepare me for the real world. State has a good record for turning out students fully prepared to take on responsibilities in the real world. It is (or isn't) a big school, but/and it has certainly taught me some big lessons about the value of (whatever personality values apply) in the real world of business."

If the interviewer has a follow-up question about the role your parents played in selection of your school, be wary—he or she is plumbing your maturity. It is best to reply that the choice of the school was yours, though you did seek the advice of your parents once you had made your decision, and that they supported your decision.

"Are you looking for a permanent or temporary job?"

The interviewer wants reassurance that you are genuinely interested in the position and won't disappear in a few months to pursue post-doctoral studies in St. Tropez. Try to go beyond saying simply yes: Explain why you want the job. You might say, "Of course, I am looking for a permanent job. I intend to make my career in this field, and I want the opportunity to learn the business, face new challenges, and learn from experienced professionals." You will also want to qualify the question with one of your own at the end of your answer: "Is this a permanent or a temporary position you are trying to fill?" And don't be scared to ask. The occasional unscrupulous employer will hire someone fresh out of school for a short period of time—say, for one particular project—and then lay them off.

"How did you pay for college?"

Avoid saying "Oh, Daddy handled all of that," as it probably won't create quite the impression you'd like. Your parents may well have helped you out, but you should explain, if it's appropriate, that you worked part-time and took out loans (as most of us must during college).

"We have tried to hire people from your school/your major before, and they never seem to work out. What makes you different?"

Here's a stress question to test your poise and analytical skills. You can shout that, yes, of course you are different and can prove it. So far, though, all you know is that there was a problem, not what caused the problem. Respond this way: "First, may I ask you exactly what problems you've had with people from this background?" Once you know what the problem is (if one really exists at all—it may just be a curve ball to test your poise) then you can illustrate how you are different. But only then. Otherwise, you run the risk of your answer being interrupted with, "Well, that's what everyone else said before I hired them. You haven't shown me that you are different."

"I'd be interested to hear about some things you learned in school that could be used on the job."

While specific job-related courses could form part of your answer, they cannot be all of it. The interviewer wants to hear about "real-world" skills, so oblige by explaining what the experience of college taught you rather than a specific course. In other words, explain how the experience honed your relevant personality profiles. "Within my major and minor I tried to pursue those courses that had most practical relevance, such as . . . However, the greatest lessons I learned were the importance of . . ." and then list your personality profile strengths.

"Do you like routine tasks/regular hours?"

A trick question. The interviewer knows from bitter experience that most recent graduates hate routine and are hopeless as employees until they come to an acceptance of such facts of life. Explain that, yes, you appreciate the need for routine, that you expect a fair amount of routine assignments before you are entrusted with the more responsible ones, and that that is why you are prepared to accept it as necessary. As far as regular hours go you could say, "No, there's no problem there. A company expects to make a profit, so the doors have 'o be open for business on a regular basis."

"What have you done that shows initiative and willingness to work?"
Again, tell a story about how you landed or created a job for yourself, or even got involved in some volunteer work. Your answer should show initiative in that you both handled unexpected problems calmly and anticipated others. Your willingness is demonstrated by the ways you overcame obstacles. For example: "I worked for a summer in a small warehouse. I found out that a large shipment was due in a couple of weeks, and I knew that room had to be made. The inventory system was outdated, and the rear of the warehouse was disorganized, so I came in on a Saturday, figured out how much room I needed, cleaned up the mess in the rear, and catalogued it all on the new inventory forms. When the shipment arrived, the truck just backed in. There was even room to spare."

Often after an effort above and beyond the call of duty, a manager might congratulate you, and if it had happened to you in this instance, you might conclude your answer with the verbal endorsement. "The divisional manager happened along just when I was finishing the job, and said he wished he had more people who took such pride in their work."

"Can you take instructions without feeling upset or hurt?"
This is a manageability question. If you take offense easily or bristle when your mistakes are pointed out, you won't last long with any company. Competition is fierce at the entry level, so take this as another chance to set yourself apart. "Yes, I can take instructions—and more important, I can take constructive criticism without feeling hurt. Even with the best intent, I will still make mistakes, and at times someone will have to put me back on the right track. I know that if I ever expect to rise in the company, I must first prove myself to be manageable."

"Have you ever had difficulties getting along with others?"
This is a combination question, probing willingness and manageability. Are you a team player or are you going to disrupt the department and make the interviewer's life miserable? This is a closed-ended question that requires only a yes/no answer, so give one and shut up.

"What type of position are you interested in?"
This again is one of those questions that tempts you to mention management. Don't. Say you are interested in what you will be offered anyway, which is an entry-level job. "I am interested in an entry-level position that will enable me to learn this business inside and out, and will give me the opportunity to grow when I prove myself, either on a professional or a managerial ladder."

"What qualifications do you have that will make you successful in this field?"
There is more to answering this question than reeling off your academic qualifications. In addition you will want to stress relevant work experience and

illustrate your strong points as they match the key personality traits as they apply to the position you seek. It's a simple, wide-open question that says, "Hey, we're looking for an excuse to hire you. Give us some help."

"Why do you think you would like this type of work?"

This is a deceptively simple question because there is no pat answer. It is usually asked to see whether you really understand what the specific job and profession entails on a day-to-day basis. So, to answer it requires you to have researched the company and job functions as carefully as possible. Preparation for this should include a call to another company in the field and a request to speak to someone doing the job you hope to get. Ask what the job is like and what that person does day to day. How does the job fit into the department? What contribution does it make to the overall efforts of the company? Why does he or she like that type of work? Armed with that information, you will show that you understand what you are getting into; most recent graduates do not.

"What's your idea of how industry works?"

The interviewer does not want a long dissertation, just the reassurance that you don't think it works along the same lines as a registered charity. Your understanding should be something like this: "The role of any company is to make as much money as possible, as quickly and efficiently as possible, and in a manner that will encourage repeat business from the existing client base and new business from word of mouth and reputation." Finish with the observation that it is every employee's role to play as a team member in order to achieve those goals.

"What do you know about our company?"

You can't answer this question unless you have enough interest to research the company thoroughly. If you don't have that interest, you should expect someone who has made the effort to get the job.

"What do you think determines progress in a good company?"

Your answer will include all the positive personality traits you have been illustrating throughout the interview. Include allusions to the listening profile, determination, ability to take the rough with the smooth, adherence to systems and procedures, and the good fortune to have a manager who wants you to grow.

"Do you think grades should be considered by first employers?"

If your grades were good, the answer is obviously yes. If they weren't, your answer needs a little more thought. "Of course, an employer should take everything into consideration, and along with grades will be an evaluation of willingness, manageability, an understanding of how business works, and actual work experience. Combined, such experience and professional skills can be more valuable than grades alone."

□□□

Many virtuous candidates are called for entry-level interviews, but only those who prepare themselves to answer the tough questions will be chosen. Interviews for recent graduates are partly sales presentations. And the more you interview, the better you get, so don't leave preparing for them until the last minute. Start now and hone your skills to get a headstart on your peers. Finally, here's what a professor from a top-notch business school once told me: "You are taking a new product to market. Accordingly, you've got to analyze what it can do, who is likely to be interested, and how you are going to sell it to them." Take some time to get to know yourself and your particular values as they will be perceived in the world of business.

18.
The Graceful Exit

To paraphrase Shakespeare, all the employment world's a stage, and all the people on it merely players making their entrances and exits. Curtains rise and fall, and your powerful performance must be capped with a professional and memorable exit. To ensure you leave the right impression, this chapter will review the dos and don'ts of leaving an interview.

A signal that the interview is drawing to a close comes when you are asked whether you have any questions. Ask questions, and by doing so, highlight your strengths and show your enthusiasm. Your goal at the interview is to generate a job offer, so you should find it easy to avoid the crimes that damage your case.

Don'ts:

1. Don't discuss salary, vacation, or benefits. It is not that the questions are invalid, just that the timing is wrong. Bringing such topics up before you have an offer is asking what the company can do for you—instead, you should be saying what you can do for the company. Those topics are part of the negotiation (handled in Chapter 21, "Negotiating the Offer"); remember, without an offer you have nothing to negotiate.

2. Don't press for an early decision. Of course, you should ask, "When will I know your decision?" But don't press it. And don't try to use the "other-opportunities-I-have-to-consider" gambit as leverage when no such offers exist—that annoys the interviewer, makes you look foolish, and may even force you to negotiate from a position of weakness. Timing is everything;

the issue of how to handle other opportunities as leverage is explored in detail later.

3. Don't show discouragement. Sometimes a job offer can occur on the spot. Usually, it does not. So don't show discouragement if you are not offered the job at the interview, because discouragement shows a lack of self-esteem and determination. Avoiding a bad impression is merely the foundation of leaving a good one, and the right image to leave is one of enthusiasm, guts, and openness—just the traits you have been projecting throughout the interview.

4. Don't ask for an evaluation of your interview performance. That forces the issue and puts the interviewer in an awkward position. You *can* say that you want the job, and ask what you have to do to get it.

Dos:

1. Ask appropriate job-related questions. When the opportunity comes to ask any final questions, review your notes. Bring up any relevant strengths that haven't been addressed.

2. Show decisiveness. If you are offered the job, react with enthusiasm. Then sleep on it. If it's possible to do so without making a formal acceptance, lock the job up now and put yourself in control; you can always change your mind later. But before you make any commitment with regard to compensation, see Chapter 21, "Negotiating the Offer."

3. When you are interviewed by more than one person, be sure you have the correct spelling of their names. "I enjoyed meeting your colleagues, Ms. Smith. Could you give me the correct spelling of their names, please?" This question will give you the names you forgot in the heat of battle and will demonstrate your consideration.

4. Review the job's requirements with the interviewer. Match them point by point with your skills and attributes.

5. Find out if this is the only interview. If so, you must ask for the job in a positive and enthusiastic manner. Find out the timeframe for a decision and finish with: "I am very enthusiastic about the job and the contributions I can make. If your decision will be made by the 15th, what must I do in the meantime to assure I get the job?"

6. Ask for the next interview. When there are subsequent interviews in the hiring procedure, ask for the next interview in the same honest and forthright manner. "Is now a good time to schedule our next meeting?" If you do not ask, you do not get.

7. Keep yourself in contention. A good leading question to ask is, "Until I hear from you again, what particular aspects of the job and this interview should I be considering?"

8. Always depart in the same polite and assured manner you entered. Look the interviewer in the eye, put on a smile (there's no need to grin), give a firm handshake, and say, "This has been an exciting meeting for me. This is a job I can do, and I feel I can contribute to your goals, because the atmosphere here seems conducive to doing my very best work. When will we speak again?"

IV

Finishing Touches

The successful completion of every interview is a big stride toward getting job offers, yet it is not the end of your job hunt.

A company rarely hires the first competent person it sees. A hiring manager will sometimes interview as many as 15 people for a particular job, but the strain and pace of conducting interviews naturally dim the memory of each applicant. Unless you are the last person to be interviewed, the impression you make will fade with each subsequent interview the interviewer undertakes. And if you are not remembered, you will not be offered the job. You must develop a strategy to keep your name and skills constantly in the forefront of the interviewer's mind. These finishing touches often make all the difference.

Some of the suggestions here may not seem earth-shattering, just simple, sensible demonstrations of your manners, enthusiasm, and determination. But remember that today all employers are looking for people with that extra little something. You can avoid the negative or merely indifferent impression and be certain of creating a positive one by following these guidelines.

19.
Out of Sight, Out of Mind

The first thing you do on leaving the interview is breathe a sigh a relief. The second is to make sure that "out of sight, out of mind" will not apply to you. You do this by starting a follow-up procedure immediately after the interview.

Sitting in your car, on the bus, train, or plane, do a written recap of the interview while it's still fresh in your mind. Answer these questions.

- Whom did you meet? (Names and titles.)
- What does the job entail?
- What are the first projects/biggest challenges?
- Why can you do the job?
- What aspects of the interview went poorly? Why?
- What is the agreed-upon next step?
- What was said during the last few minutes of the interview?

Probably the most difficult—and most important—thing to do is to analyze what aspects of the interview went poorly. A person does not get offered a job based solely on strength. On the contrary, many people get new jobs based on their relative lack of negatives as compared to the other applicants. So, it is mandatory that you look for and recognize any negatives from your performance. That is the only way you will have an opportunity to package and overcome those negatives in your follow-up procedure and during subsequent interviews.

The next step is to write the follow-up letter to the interviewer to acknowledge the meeting and to keep you fresh in his or her mind. Writing a follow-up letter also shows that you are both appreciative and organized, and it refreshes the urgency of your candidacy at the expense of other candidates. But remember that a canned follow-up form letter could hurt your candidacy.

☐ **1. Type the letter.** It exhibits greater professionalism. If you don't own a typewriter, the local library will frequently allow the use of theirs. If not, a typing service will do it for a nominal fee. If, for any reason, the letter cannot be typed, make sure it is legibly and neatly written. The letter should make four points clear to the company representative:

- you paid attention to what was being said;
- you understood the importance of the interviewer's comments;
- you are excited about the job, can do it, and want it;
- you can contribute to those first major projects.

☐ **2. Use the right words and phrases in your letter.** Here are some you might want to use.

- "Upon reflection," or, "Having thought about our meeting . . ."
- Recognize—"I recognize the importance of . . ."
- Listen—"Listening to the points you made . . ."
- Enthusiasm—Let the interviewer catch your enthusiasm. It is very effective, especially as your letter will arrive while other applicants are nervously sweating their way through the interview.
- Impressed—Let the interviewer know you were impressed with the people/product/service/facility/market/position, but do not overdo it.
- Challenge—Show that you feel you would be challenged to do your best work in this environment.
- Confidence—There is a job to be done and a challenge to be met. Let the interviewer know you are confident of doing both well.
- Interest—If you want the job (or next interview), say so. At this stage, the company is buying and you are selling. Ask for the job in a positive and enthusiastic manner.

- Appreciation—As a courtesy and mark of professional manners, you must express appreciation for the time the interviewer took out of his or her busy schedule.

☐ **3. Whenever possible and appropriate, mention the names of the people you met at the interview.** Draw attention to one of the topics that was of general interest to the interviewers.

☐ **4. Address the follow-up letter to the main interviewer.** Send a copy to personnel with a note of thanks as a courtesy.

☐ **5. Don't gild the lily.** Keep it short—less than one page—and don't make any wild claims that might not withstand close scrutiny.

☐ **6. Mail the letter within 24 hours of the interview.** If the decision is going to be made in the next couple of days, hand-deliver the letter or make a strong point by sending a mailgram. The follow-up letter will help to set you apart from other applicants and will refresh your image in the mind of the interviewer just when it would normally be starting to dim.

☐ **7. If you do not hear anything after five days (which is quite normal), put in a telephone call to the company representative.** Reiterate the points made in the letter, saying that you want the job (or next interview), and finish your statements with a question: "Mr. Smith, I feel confident about my ability to contribute to your department's efforts, and I really want the job. Could you tell me what I have to do to get it?" Then be quiet and wait for the answer.

☐☐☐

Of course, you may be told you are no longer in the running. The next chapter will show you that that is a great opportunity to snatch victory from the jaws of defeat.

20.
Snatching Victory from the Jaws of Defeat

During the interviewing process, there are bound to be interviewers who erroneously come to the conclusion that you are not the right person for the job they need to fill. When that happens, you will be turned down. Such an absurd travesty of justice can occur in different ways:

- at the interview;
- in a letter of rejection;
- during your follow-up telephone call.

Whenever the turn-down comes, you must be emotionally and intellectually prepared to take advantage of the opportunity being offered to you.

When you get turned down for the only opportunity you have going, the rejection can be devastating to your ego. That is why I have stressed the wisdom of having at least a few interviews in process at the same time.

You will get turned down. No one can be right for every job. The right person for a job doesn't always get it, however—the best prepared and most determined often does. While you may be responsible in part for the initial rejection, you still have the power to correct the situation and win the job offer. What you do with the claimed victory is a different matter—you will then be in a seller's market with choice and control of your situation.

To turn around a turn-down often requires only willpower and determination. Almost every job you desire is obtainable once you understand the hiring process from the interviewer's side of the desk. Your initial—and temporary—rejection is attributable to one of these reasons:

- interviewer does not feel you can do the job;

- interviewer feels you lack a successful profile;

- interviewer did not feel your personality would contribute to the smooth functioning of the department—perhaps you didn't portray yourself as either a team player, or as someone willing to take the extra step.

With belief in yourself, you can still succeed. Repeat to yourself constantly through the interview cycle: "I will get this job, because no one else can give as much to this company as I can!" Do that and implement the following plan immediately when you hear of rejection, whether in person, via mail, or over the telephone.

☐ **Step One:** Thank the interviewer for the time and consideration. Then ask politely: "To help my future job search, why wasn't I chosen for the position?" Assure the interviewer that you would truly appreciate an honest, objective analysis. Listen to the reply and do not interrupt regardless of the comments. Use your time constructively and take notes furiously. When the company representative finishes speaking, show you understood the comments. (Remember, understanding and agreeing are different animals.)

"Thank you, Mr. Smith, now I can understand the way you feel. Because I am not a professional interviewer, I'm afraid my interview nerves got in the way. I'm very interested in working for your company" [use an enthusiastic tone] "and am determined to get the job. Let me meet with you once again. This time, when I'm not so nervous, I am confident you will see I really do have the skills you require" [then provide an example of a skill you have in the questionable area]. "You name the time and the place, and I will be there. What's best for you, Mr. Smith?"

End with a question, of course. An enthusiastic request like that is very difficult to refuse and will usually get you another interview. An interview, of course, at which you must shine.

☐ **Step Two:** Check your notes and accept the company representative's concerns. Their validity is irrelevant; the important point is that the negative points represent the problem areas in the interviewer's perception of you. List the negative perceptions, and using the techniques, exercises, and value keys discussed throughout the book, develop different ways to overcome or compensate for every negative perception.

☐ **Step Three:** Re-read section III.

☐ **Step Four:** Practice aloud the statements and responses you will use at the interview. If you can practice with someone who plays the part of the interviewer, so much the better. That will create a real interview atmosphere and be helpful to your success. Lacking a role-play partner, you can create that live answer by putting the anticipated objections and questions on a tape and responding to them.

☐ **Step Five:** Study all available information on the company.

☐ **Step Six:** Congratulate yourself continually for getting another interview after initial rejection. This is proof of your self-worth, ability, and tenacity. You have nothing to lose and everything to gain, having already risen phoenix-like from the ashes of temporary defeat.

☐ **Step Seven:** During the interview, ask for the job in a positive and enthusiastic manner. Your drive and staying power will impress the interviewer. All you must do to win the job is overcome the perceived negatives, and you have been given the time to prepare. Go for it.

☐ **Step Eight:** Even when all has failed at the subsequent interview, do not leave without a final request for the job. Play your trump card: "Mr. Smith, I respect the fact that you allowed me the opportunity to prove myself here today. I am convinced I am the best person for the job. I want you to give me a trial, and I will prove on the job that I am the best hiring decision you have made this year. Will you give us both the opportunity?"

A reader wrote to me as I was revising *Knock 'em Dead* for this new edition. The letter read in part, "I read the chapter entitled 'Snatching Victory from the Jaws of Defeat' and did everything you said to salvage what appeared to be a losing interview. My efforts did make a very good impression on the interviewer, but as it was finally explained to me, I really did not have equal qualifications for the job, and finally came in a close second. I really want to work for this growing company, and they say they have another position coming up in six months. What should I do?"

I know of someone in the airline business who wanted a job working on that most prestigious of aircraft, the Concorde. He had been recently laid off and had high hopes for a successful interview. As it happened, he came in second for the Concorde position. He was told that the firm would speak to him again in the near future. So he waited—for eight months. Finally, he realized that waiting for the job could only leave him unemployed. The moral of the story is that you must be brutally objective when you come out second-best and, whatever the interviewer says, you must sometimes assume that you are getting the polite brush-off.

With that in mind, let's see what can be done on the positive side. First of all, send a thank-you note to the interviewer, acknowledging your understanding of the state of affairs and re-affirming your desire to work for the company. Conclude with a polite request to bear you in mind for the future.

Then, keep an eye out for any news item about the company in the press. Whenever you see something, cut it out and mail it to the interviewer with a very brief note that says something like: "I came across this in *Forbes* and thought you might find it interesting. I am still determined to be your next account manager, so please keep me in mind when the next opening occurs."

You can also call the interviewer once every couple of months, just to check in. Remember, of course, to keep the phone call brief and polite—you simply want to keep your name at the top of the interviewer's mind.

And maybe something will come of it. Ultimately, however, your only choice is to move on. There is no gain waiting on an interviewer's word. Go out and keep looking, because chances are that you will come up with an even better job. Then, if you still want to work for that company that gave you the brush-off, you will have some leverage.

Most people fail in their endeavors by quitting just before the dawn of success. Follow these directions and you can win the job. You have proved yourself to be a fighter and that is universally admired. The company representative will want you to succeed because you are made of stuff that is rarely seen today. You are a person of guts, drive, and endurance—the hallmarks of a winner. Job turndowns are an opportunity to exercise and build your strengths, and by persisting, you may well add to your growing number of job offers, now and in the future.

21.
Negotiating the Offer

The crucial period after you have been made a formal offer, and before you accept, is probably the one point in your relationship with an employer that you can say with any accuracy that you have the whip hand. The advantage, for now, is yours. They want you but don't have you; and their wanting something they don't have gives you a negotiating edge. An employer is also more inclined to respect and honor a person who has a clear understanding of his or her worth in the marketplace—they want a savvy and businesslike person.

Job offers and negotiations usually begin with talk of money, but that isn't where they should end. You don't have to accept or reject the first offer, whatever it is. In most instances, you can improve on the initial offer in a number of ways.

First, you must find out what you're worth.

☐ **Step One:** Before getting into negotiation with any employer, work out your minimum cash requirements for any job. Prior to getting into serious money discussions, you must know what it is going to take to keep a roof over your head and bread on the table. You need to know that figure, but you don't ever have to discuss it with anyone—knowing it is the foundation of getting both what you need and what you are worth.

☐ **Step Two:** Get a grip on what your skills are worth in the current market. There are a number of ways to do that. Consider the resources and methods outlined below.

- You may be able to find out the salary range for the level above you and the level beneath you at the company in question.

- You can get information from the Bureau of Labor Statistics in Washington, DC, which keeps stats on hundreds of job titles. Be warned, however, that those titles are often a little to a lot out of date.

- Your state labor office may have salary ranges available for you to review.

- Ask headhunters—they know better than anyone what the market will bear. You should, as a matter of career prudence, establish an ongoing relationship with a reputable headhunter, because you never know when his or her services will come in handy.

- Many professional journals publish annual salary surveys you can consult.

- *The National Business Employment Weekly*, a magazine published by the *Wall Street Journal*, carries hundreds of positions in the professions every week and will quickly give you a handle on the going rates. It contains timely articles on job-hunting techniques as well.

In short, find out the minimum you can live on, and find out the going rate in today's marketplace. The first is for your personal consumption and unlikely ever to be raised in your negotiations. The second is for the negotiation time, so that your real area of discussion is, "What is this job worth to the employer?"

Negotiate When You Can

I have said throughout *Knock 'em Dead* that your sole aim at the interview is to get the job offer, because without it you have nothing to negotiate. Once the offer is extended, the time to negotiate has arrived, and there will never be a more opportune time. Your relationship with the potential employer has gone through a number of distinct changes—from, "Perhaps we should speak to this one," to, "Yes, he might be able to do the job," through, "This is the top candidate, we really like him and want to have him on board." But now is the only point in the relationship when you will have the upper hand. Enjoy it while you can.

The salary you accept for your next job will affect your earning capabilities for many years to come. A lack of negotiating savvy now that costs, say, $2000 for a thirty-year-old turns into $70,000 by the time he or she reaches retirement—and even more when you consider that every salary review based on the higher negotiated salary would make lifetime earnings that much greater.

Although questions of salary are usually brought up after you are under serious consideration, you must be careful to avoid painting yourself into a corner when you fill out the initial company application form that contains a request for required salary. Usually you can get away with "open" as a response; sometimes the form will instruct you not to write "open," in which case you can write "negotiable," or "competitive."

So much for basic considerations. Let's move on to the money questions that are likely to be flying around the room.

The salary/job negotiation begins in earnest in two ways. The interviewer can bring up the topic with statements like:

- "How do you think you would like working here?"

- "People with your background always fit in well with us."

- "You could make a real contribution here."

- "Well, you certainly seem to have what it takes."

Or, if it is clearly appropriate to do so, you can bring on the negotiating stage. In that case, you can make mirror images of the above, which make the interviewer face the fact that you certainly are able to do the job, and that the time has therefore come to talk turkey:

- "How do you think I would fit in with the group?"

- "I feel my background and experience would definitely complement the workgroup, don't you?"

- "I think I could make a real contribution here. What do you think?"

- "I know I have what it takes to do this job. What questions are lingering in your mind?"

Now then. What do you do when the question of money is brought up before you have enough details about the job to negotiate from a position of knowledge and strength? Postpone money talk until you have the facts in hand. Do that by asking something like: "I still have one or two questions about my responsibilities, and it will be easier for me to talk about money when I have cleared them up. Could I first ask you a few questions about . . . ?"

Then proceed to clarify duties and responsibilities, being careful to weigh the relative importance of the position and the individual duties to the success of the department you may join.

The employer is duty-bound to get your services as reasonably as possible, while you have an equal responsibility to do the best you can for yourself. Your goal is not to settle for less than will enable you to be happy on the job—unhappiness at work can taint the rest of your life. It is far easier to negotiate down than it is to negotiate up. The value of the offer you accept depends on your performance throughout the interview and hiring cycle, and especially the finesse you display in the final negotiations. The rest of the chapter is going to address the many questions that might be asked, or that you might ask, to bring matters to a successful conclusion.

"What is an adequate reward for your efforts?"

A glaring manageability question and money probe all in one. The interviewer probably already has a typist on staff who expects a Nobel Prize each time he or she gets out a faultless letter. Your answer should be honest and cover all bases. "My primary satisfaction and reward comes from a job well done and completed on time. The occasional good word from my boss is always welcome. Last but not least, I think everyone looks forward to a salary review."

"What is your salary history?" or, "What was your salary progress on your last job?"

The interviewer is looking for a couple of things here. First, he or she is looking for the frequency, percentage, and dollar-value of your raises, which in turn tell him or her about your performance and the relative value of the offer that is about to be made. What you want to avoid is tying the potential offer to your salary history—the offer you negotiate should be based solely on the value of the job in hand. That is even more important if you are a woman, because the statistics tell us that women are still paid less than their male counterparts for equal work.

Your answer needs to be specifically vague. Perhaps: "My salary history has followed a steady upward path, and I have never failed to receive merit increases. I would be glad to give you the specific numbers if needed, but I shall have to sit down and give it some thought with a pencil and paper." The odds are that the interviewer will not ask you to do that; if he or she does, nod in agreement and say that you'll get right to it when you get home. Don't begin the task until you are requested a second time, which is unlikely.

If for any reason you do get your back against the wall with this one, be sure to include in the specifics of your answer that "one of the reasons I am leaving my current job is that raises were standard for all levels of employees, so that despite my superior contributions, I got the same percentage raise as the tardy employee. I want to work in an environment where I will be recognized and rewarded for my contributions." Then end with a question: "Is this the sort of company where I can expect that?"

"What were you making on your last job?"

A similar but different question. It could also be phrased, "What are you making now?" or, "What is your current salary?"

While I have said that your current earnings should bear no relation to your starting salary on the new job, it can be difficult to make that statement clear to the interviewer without appearing objectionable. Although the question asks you to be specific, you needn't get too specific. Instead, you should try to draw attention to the fact that the two jobs are different. A short answer might include: "I am earning $X, although I'm not sure how that will help you in your evaluation of my worth for this job, because the two jobs are somewhat different."

It is important to understand the "areas of allowable fudge." For instance, if you are considerably underpaid, you may want to weigh the dollar-value of such perks as medical and dental plans, pay in lieu of vacation, profit-sharing and pension plans, bonuses, stock options, and other incentives. For many people, those can add between 20 to 35 percent to their base salary—you might honestly be able to mention a higher figure than you at first thought possible. Also, if you are due for a raise imminently, you are justified in adding it in.

It isn't common for current or previous salaries to be verified by employers, although certain industries, because of legal requirements, check more than others do (for instance, the stock market or the liquor business).

Before your "current salary" disappears through the roof, however, you should know that the interviewer can ask to see a payroll stub or W2 form at the time you start work, or could make the offer dependent on verification of salary. After you are hired, the new employer may request verbal or written confirmation from previous employers, or might use an outside verification agency. In any instance where the employer contacts someone verbally or in writing, the employer must by law have your written permission to do so. That small print on the bottom of the job application form followed by a request for your signature usually authorizes the employer to do just that.

"Have you ever been refused a salary increase?"
This implies that you asked. An example of your justifiable request might parallel the following true story. An accountant in a tire distributorship made changes to an accounting system that saved $65,000 a year, plus 30 staff hours a week. Six months after the methods were obviously working smoothly, he requested a salary review, was refused, but was told he would receive a year-end bonus. He did: $75. If you can tell a story like that, by all means tell how you were turned down for a raise. If not, it is best to play it safe and explain that your work and salary history showed a steady and marked continual improvement over the years.

"How much do you need to support your family?"
This question is sometimes asked of people who will be working in a sales job, where remuneration is based upon a draw against forthcoming commissions. If that describes your income patterns, be sure you have a firm handle on your basic needs.

For salaried positions, this question is of questionable relevance. It implies the employer will try to get you at a subsistence salary, which is not why you are there. In this instance, give a range from your desired high-end salary down to your desired mid-point salary.

"How much will it take to get you?" "How much are you looking for?" "What are your salary expectations?" "What are your salary requirements?"

You are being asked to name a figure here. Give the wrong answer and you can get eliminated. It is always a temptation to ask for the moon, knowing you can come down later, but there are better approaches. It is wise to confirm your understanding of the job and its importance before you start throwing numbers around, because you will have to live with the consequences. You need the best possible offer without pricing yourself out of the market, so it's time to dance with one of the following responses.

"Well, let's see if I understand the responsibilities fully . . ." You then proceed to itemize exactly what you will be doing on a daily basis and the parameters of your responsibilities and authority. Once that is done you will seek agreement: "Is this the job as you see it or have I missed anything?" Remember to describe the job in its most flattering and challenging light, paying special attention to the way you see it fitting into the overall picture and contributing to the success of department, workgroup, and company. You can then finish your response with a question of your own: "What figure did you have in mind for someone with my track record?" or, "What range has been authorized for this position?" Your answer will include, in part, something along the lines of, "I believe my skills and experience will warrant a starting salary between _____ and _____."

You also could ask, "What would be the salary range for someone with my experience and skills?" or, "I naturally want to make as much as my background and skills will allow. If I am right for the job, and I think my credentials demonstrate that I am, I am sure you will make me a fair offer. What figure do you have in mind?"

Another good response is: "I would expect a salary appropriate to my experience and ability to do the job successfully. What range do you have in mind?"

Such questions will get the interviewer to reveal the salary range, and concentrate his or her attention on the challenges of the job and your ability to accept and work with those challenges.

When you are given a range, you can adjust your money requirements appropriately, latching on to the upper part of the range. For example, if the range is $30,000-$35,000 a year, you can come back with a range of $34,000-$37,000.

$$\left.\begin{matrix} 30 \\ \\ 35 \end{matrix}\right[\qquad \left.\begin{matrix} 34 \\ \\ 37 \end{matrix}\right]$$

Consequently, your response will include: "That certainly means we have something to talk about. While your range is $30,000-$35,000, I am looking for a minimum of $34,000 with an ideal of $37,000. Tell me, what flexibility is there at the top of your salary range?" You need to know to put yourself in the strongest negotiating position, and this is the perfect time and opportunity to gain the information and the advantage.

All this fencing is aimed at getting the interviewer to show his or her hand first. Ask for too much, and it's "Oh dear, I'm afraid you're overqualified"–to which you can reply, "So overpay me." (Actually, that works when you can carry it off with an ingratiating smile.) If your request is too low, you are likely to be ruled out as lacking the appropriate experience.

When you have tried to get the interviewer to name a range and failed, you must come up with specific dollars and cents. At this point, the key is to understand that all jobs have salary ranges attached to them. Consequently, the last thing you will ever do is come back with a specific dollar figure–that traps you. Instead, you will mention your own range, which will not be from your minimum to your maximum but rather from your midpoint to your maximum. Remember, you can always negotiate down, but can rarely negotiate up.

"What kind of salary are you worth?"

This is a how-much-do-you-want question with a slight twist. It is asking you to name a desired figure, but the twist is that it also asks you to justify that figure. It requires that you demonstrate careful analysis of your worth, industry norms, and job requirements. You are recommended to try for a higher figure rather than a lower one. "Having compared my background and experience with industry norms and salary surveys, I feel my general worth is in the region of $X to $Y. My general background and credentials fit your needs, and my first-hand knowledge of the specific challenges and projects I would face in this job are an exact match, so I feel worthy of justifying an offer towards the top of this range. Don't you agree?"

After your response to a salary question, you can expect to hear, "That's too much," or, "Oh, that is more than we were hoping to pay," or, "That would be stretching the budget to the breaking point." When that happens, accept it as no more than a negotiating gambit and come back with your own calm rebuttal: "What did you have in mind?"

"What do you hope to be earning two to five years from now?"

A difficult question. The interviewer is probing your desired career and earning path and is trying to see whether you have your sights set high enough– or too high. Perhaps a jocular tone doesn't hurt here: "I'd like to be earning just about as much as my boss and I can work out!" Then, throw the ball back with your own question: "How much is it possible to make here?"

If you give a specific figure, the interviewer is going to want justification. If you come up with a salary range, you are advised also to have a justified career path to go along with it.

You could also say, "In two years, I will have finished my C.P.A. requirements, so with that plus my additional experience, industry norms say I should be earning between $X and $Y. I would hope to be earning at least within that range, but hopefully with a proven track record of contributions, I would be making above the norm." The trick is to use industry statistics as the backbone of your argument, express confidence in doing better than the norm, and whenever possible stay away from specific job titles unless pressed.

"Do you think people in your occupation should be paid more?"
This one can be used prior to serious salary negotiation to probe your awareness of how your job really contributes to the bottom line. Or it can occur in the middle of salary negotiations to throw you off balance. The safe and correct answer is to straddle the fence. "Most jobs have salary ranges that reflect the job's relative importance and contribution to a company. And those salary ranges reflect the norm for the great majority of people within that profession. That does not mean, however, that the extraordinary people in such a group are not recognized for the extra performance and skills. There are always exceptions to the rule."

Good Offers, Poor Offers
After a period of bantering back and forth like this, the interviewer names a figure, hopefully meant as a legitimate offer. If you aren't sure, qualify it: "Let me see if I understand you correctly: Are you formally offering me the position at $X a year?"
The formal offer can fall into one of two categories.

☐ **It sounds fair and equitable:** In that case, you still want to negotiate for a little more—employers almost expect it of you, so don't disappoint them. Mention a salary range again, the low end of which comes a little below their offer and the high end somewhat above it. You can say, "Well it certainly seems that we are close. I was hoping for something more in the range of $X to $Y. How much room do we have for negotiation here?"
No one will withdraw an offer because you say you feel you are worth more. After all, the interviewer thinks you are the best person for the job, and has extended a formal offer, and the last thing he or she needs now is to start from square one again. The employer has a vested interest in bringing the negotiation to a satisfactory conclusion. In a worst-case scenario, the interviewer can stick to the original offer.

☐ **It isn't quite what you expected:** Even if the offer isn't what you thought it would be, you still have options other than accepting or rejecting the offer as it stands. But your strategy for now is to run the money topic as far as you can in a calm and businesslike way; then once you have gone that far, you can back off and examine the other potential benefits of the job. That way you will leave yourself with an opening, if you need it, to hit the money topic once more at the close of negotiations.

If you feel the salary could do with a boost, say so. "I like the job, and I know I have what it takes to be successful in it. I would also be prepared to give you a start date of [e.g.] March 1 to show my sincerity. But quite honestly, I couldn't justify it with your initial salary offer. I just hope that we have some room for negotiation here."

Or you can say, "I could start on March 1, and I do feel I could make a contribution here and become an integral part of the team. The only thing standing in the way is my inability to make ends meet based on your initial offer. I am sincerely interested in the opportunity and flattered by your interest in me. If we could just solve this money problem, I'm sure we could come to terms. What do you think can be done about it?"

The interviewer will probably come back with a question asking how much you want. "What is the minimum you would be prepared to work for?" he or she might ask. Respond with your range again—with your minimum really your midpoint—and the interviewer may well then come back with a higher offer and ask for your concurrence. This is the time to be noncommittal but encouraged, and to move on to the benefits included with the position: "Well, yes, that is a little better. Perhaps we should talk about the benefits."

Alternatively, the interviewer may come back with another question: "That's beyond our salary range for this job title. How far can you reduce your salary needs to fit our range?"

That question shows good faith and a desire to close the deal, but don't give in too easily—the interviewer is never going to want you as much as he or she does now. Your first response might be: "I appreciate that, but if it is the job title and its accompanying range that is causing the problem, couldn't we upgrade the title, thereby putting me near the bottom of the next range?" Try it—it often works. If is doesn't, it is probably time to move to other negotiable aspects of the job offer.

But not before one last try. You can take that final stab by asking, "Is that the best you can do?" With this question, you must look the interviewer directly in the eye, ask the question, and maintain eye contact. It works surprisingly well. You should also remember to try it as a closing gambit *at the very end of negotiations* when you have received everything you can hope for. You may get a surprise.

Negotiating Your Future Salary

At this point, you have probably ridden present salary as hard as you reasonably can (for a while, anyway)—so the time has come to shift the conversation to future remuneration.

"Even though the offer isn't quite what I'd hoped for to start the job, I am still interested. Can we talk about the future for a while?" Then you move the conversation to an on-the-job focus. Here are a few arrangements corporate headhunters frequently negotiate for their recruits.

☐ **A single, lump-sum signing bonus.** Nice to have, though it is money here today and gone tomorrow. Don't make the mistake of adding it onto the base. If you get a $2,500 signing bonus, that money won't be figured in for your year-end review—your raise will be based on your actual salary, so the bonus is a little less meaningful than it appears.

☐ **A 60-, 90-, or 120-day performance review with raise attached.** You can frequently negotiate a minimum percentage increase here, if you have confidence in your abilities.

☐ **A title promotion and raise** after two, three or four months.

☐ **Bonus.** When you hear talk about a year-end bonus, don't rely on "what it's going to be this year" or "what it was last year" because the actual bonus will never bear any resemblance to either figure. Base the realism of any bonus expectations on a five-year performance history.

☐ **Things other than cash.** Also in the realm of real disposable income are things like a company car, gas, maintenance, and insurance. They represent hard dollars you would not have to spend. It's not unusual to hear of employers paying car or insurance allowances, picking up servicing bills for your personal automobile, or paying gas up to a certain amount each month. But if you don't ask, you can never expect an employer to offer. What have you got to lose? Remember, though, to get any of those unusual goodies in writing—even respectable managers in respected companies can suffer amnesia.

Questions to Leverage and Evaluate the Offer

No two negotiations are going to be alike, so there is no absolute model you can follow. Nevertheless, when you have addressed present and future remuneration, this might be the time to get some more information on the company and the job itself.

Even if you haven't agreed on money, you probably are beginning to get a feeling as to whether or not you can put the deal together; you know the employer wants to. Many of the following questions will be appropriate here; some might even be appropriate at other times during the interview cycle.

Full knowledge of all the relevant facts is critical to your successful final negotiation of money and benefits. Your prudent selection of questions from this list will help you negotiate the best offers and choose the right job for you. (At this point, asking some pertinent questions from the following list also serves as a decompression device of sorts for both parties.)

☐☐☐

The questions come in these categories:

- nuts-and-bolts job clarification;
- job and department growth;
- corporate culture;
- company growth and direction

The following section is also worth reading between first and second interviews.

Nuts and Bolts

First, if you have career aspirations, you want to land in an outfit that believes in promoting from within. To find out, ask a few of these questions.

How long has the job been open? Why is it open? Who held the job last? What is he doing now? Promoted, fired, quit? How long was he in that job? How many people have held this job in the last three years? Where are they now? How often and how many people have been promoted from this position—and to where?

Other questions that might follow would include . . .

"What is the timetable for filling the position?"

The longer the job has been open and the tighter the timeframe for filling it, the better your leverage. That can also be determined by asking, "When do you need me to start? Why on that date particularly?"

"What are the first projects to be addressed?" or, "What are the major problems to be tackled and conquered?"

"What do you consider the five most important day-to-day responsibilities of this job? Why?"

"What personality traits do you consider critical to success in this job?"

"How do you see me complementing the existing group?"

"Will I be working with a team, or on my own? What will be my responsibilities as a team member? What will be my leadership responsibilities?"

"How much overtime is involved?"

"How much travel is involved?" and, "How much overnight travel?"

With overnight travel you need to find out the number of days per week and month; and more important, whether you will be paid for weekend days or given comp time. I have known companies who regularly expect you to get home from a long weekend trip at one o'clock in the morning and be at work at 8:30 on Monday—all without extra pay or comp time.

"How frequent are performance and salary reviews? And what are they based on—standard raises for all, or are they weighted toward merit and performance?

How does the performance appraisal and reward system work? Exactly how are outstanding employees recognized, judged, and rewarded?"

"What is the complete financial package for someone at my level?"

Job and Department Growth

Not everyone wants a career path—in fact, careers and career paths are fairly new to business and are a phenomenon of the latter part of the 20th century. The fast track may or may not be for you. Gauging the potential for professional growth in a job is very important for some; for others, it comes slightly lower down the list. Even if you aren't striving to head the corporation in the next few years, you will still want to know what the promotional and growth expectations are so that you don't end up with a company expecting you to scale the heights.

"To what extent are the functions of the department recognized as important and worthy of review by upper management?"

If upper management takes an interest in the doings of your workgroup, rest assured you are in a visible position for recognition and reward.

"Where and how does my department fit into the company pecking order?"

"What does the department hope to achieve in the next two to three years? How will that help the company? How will it be recognized by the company?"

"What do you see as the strengths of the department? What do you see as weaknesses that you are looking to turn into strengths?"

"What role would you hope I would play in these goals?"

"What informal/formal benchmarks will you use to measure my effectiveness and contributions?"

"Based on my effectiveness, how long would you anticipate me holding this position? When my position and responsibilities change, what are the possible titles and responsibilities I might grow into?"

"What is the official corporate policy on internal promotion? How many people in this department have been promoted from their original positions since joining the company?"

"How do you determine when a person is ready for promotion?"

"What training and professional development programs are available to help me grow professionally?"

"Does the company encourage outside professional development training? Does the company sponsor all or part of any costs?"

"What are my potential career paths within the company?"

"To what jobs have people with my title risen in the company?"

"Who in the company was in this position the shortest length of time? Why? Who has remained in this position the longest? Why?"

Corporate Culture

All companies have their own way of doing things—that's corporate culture. Not every corporate culture is for you.

"What is the company's mission? What are the company's goals?"

"What approach does this company take to its marketplace?"

"What is unique about the way this company operates?"

"What is the best thing you know about this company? What is the worst thing you know about this company?"

"How does the reporting structure work? What are the accepted channels of communication and how do they work?"

"What kinds of checks and balances, reports, or other work-measurement tools are used in the department and company?"

"What do you and the company consider important in my fitting into the corporate culture—the way of doing things around here?"

"Will I be encouraged or discouraged from learning about the company beyond my own department?"

Company Growth and Direction

For those concerned about career growth, a healthy company is mandatory; for those concerned about stability of employment, the same applies.

"What expansion is planned for this department, division, or facility?"

"What markets does the company anticipate developing?"

"Does the company have plans for mergers or acquisitions?"

"Currently, what new endeavors is the company actively pursuing?"

"How do market trends affect company growth and progress? What is being done about them?"

"What production and employee layoffs and cutbacks have you experienced in the last three years?"

"What production and employee layoffs and cutbacks do you anticipate? How are they likely to affect this department, division, or facility?"

"When was the last corporate reorganization? How did it affect this department? When will the next corporate re-organization occur? How will it affect this department?"

"Is this department a profit center? How does that affect remuneration?"

The Package

Take-home pay is the most important part of your package. (You'll probably feel that the only thing wrong with your pay is that it gets taxed before you get to take it home!) That means you must carefully negotiate any possible benefits accruing to the job that have a monetary value but are nontaxable, and/or add to your physical and mental happiness. The list is almost endless, but here is a comprehensive listing of commonly available benefits. Although many of these benefits are available to all employees at some companies, you should know that, as a rule of thumb, the higher up the ladder you climb, the more benefits you can expect. Because the corporate world and its concepts of creating a motivated and committed workforce are constantly in flux, you should never assume that a particular benefit will not be available to you.

The basic rule is to ask—if you don't ask, there is no way you will get. A few years ago, it would have been unthinkable that anyone but an executive could expect something as glamorous as an athletic-club membership in a benefits package. In the 1990s, however, more companies have a membership as a standard benefit; an increasing number are even building their own health-club facilities. In New York you can easily pay between $250 and $700 for membership in a good club. What's this benefit worth in your area? Call a club and find out.

Benefits Your Package May Include

- 401K and other investment matching programs;
- cafeteria insurance plans—you pick the insurance benefits you want;
- car allowance;
- car insurance or an allowance;
- car maintenance and gas or an allowance;
- car;
- compensation days—for unpaid overtime/business travel time;
- country-club or health-club membership;
- accidental death insurance;
- deferred compensation;
- dental insurance—note deductibles and the percentage that is employer-paid;
- employment contract and/or termination contract;
- expense account;
- financial planning help and tax assistance;

- life insurance;

- medical insurance—note deductibles and percentage that is employer-paid;

- optical insurance—note deductibles and percentage that is employer-paid;

- paid sick leave;

- pension plans;

- personal days off;

- profit sharing;

- short- or long-term disability compensation plans;

- stock options;

- vacation.

Evaluating the Offer

Once the offer has been negotiated to the best of your ability, you need to evaluate it—and that doesn't have to be done on the spot. Some of your requests and questions will take time to get answered, and very often the final parts of negotiation—"Yes, Mr. Jones, we can give you the extra $20,000 and six months of vacation you requested"—will take place over the telephone. Regardless of where the final negotiations are completed, never accept or reject the offer on the spot.

Be positive, say how excited you are about the prospect and that you would like a little time (overnight, a day, two days) to think it over, discuss it with your spouse, consult your tarot cards, whatever. Not only is this delay standard practice, but it will also give you the opportunity to leverage other offers, as discussed in the next chapter.

Use the time you gain to speak to your mentors or advisors. But a word of caution: In asking advice from those close to you, be sure you know exactly where that advice is coming from—you need clear-headed objectivity at this time.

Once the advice is in, and not before, weigh it along with your own observations—no one knows your needs and aspirations better than you do. While there are many ways of doing that, a simple line down the middle of a sheet of paper, with the reasons to take the job written on one side and the reasons to turn it down on the other, is about as straightforward and objective as you can get.

You will weigh salary, future earnings and career prospects, benefits, commute, lifestyle, and stability of the company, along with all those intangibles that are summed up in the term gut feelings. Make sure you answer these questions for yourself:

- Do you like the work?

- Can you be trained in a reasonable period of time, thus having a realistic chance of success on the job?

- Are the title and responsibilities likely to provide you with challenge?

- Is the opportunity for growth in the job compatible with your needs and desires?

- Is the company location, stability, and reputation in line with your needs?

- Is the atmosphere/culture of the company conducive to you enjoying working at the company?

- Can you get along with your new manager and immediate workgroup?

- Is the money offer and total compensation package the best you can get?

Notice that money is but one aspect of the evaluation process. There are many other factors to take into account as well. Even a high-paying job can be less advantageous than you think. For instance, you should be careful not to be foxed by the gross figure. It really is important that you get a firm handle on those actual, spendable, after-tax dollars—the ones with which you pay the rent. Always look at an offer in the light of how many more spendable dollars a week it will put in your pocket.

Evaluating the New Boss

When all that is done, you must make a final but immensely important determination—whether or not you will be happy with your future manager. Remember, you are going to spend the majority of your waking hours at work, and the new job can only be as good as your relationship with your new boss. If you felt uncomfortable with the person after an interview or two, you need to evaluate carefully the kind of discomfort and unhappiness it could generate over the coming months and years.

You'll want to know about the manager's personal style: Is he or she confrontational, authoritarian, democratic, hands-off? How would reprimands or differing viewpoints be handled? Does he or she share information on a need-to-know basis, the old military-management style of keep-'em-in-the-dark? When a group member makes a significant contribution, who gets the credit as far as senior management is concerned—the person, the manager, or the group? You can find out some of that information from the manager; other aspects you'll need to review when you meet team members, or from personnel.

Accepting New Jobs, Resigning from Others

Once your decision is made, you should accept the job verbally. Spell out exactly what you are accepting: "Mr. Smith, I'd like to accept the position of engineer at a starting salary of $42,000. I will be able to start work on March 1. And I understand my package will include life, health, and dental insurance, a 401K plan, and a company car." Then you finish with: "I will be glad to start on the above date pending a written offer received in time to give my present employer adequate notice of my departure. I'm sure that's acceptable to you."

Until you have the offer in writing, you have nothing. A verbal offer can be withdrawn—it happens all the time. That's not because the employer suddenly doesn't like you, but because of reasons that affect, but bear no real relationship to your candidacy. I have known of countless careers that have stalled through reneged verbal offers—they lead to unemployment, bitterness, and even lawsuits. So avoid the headaches and play it by the numbers.

Once you have the offer in writing, notify your current employer in the same fashion. Quitting is difficult for almost everyone, so you can write a pleasant resignation letter, walk into your boss's office, hand it to him or her, then discuss things calmly and pleasantly once he or she has read it.

You will also want to notify any other companies who have been in negotiation with you that you are no longer on the market, but that you were most impressed with meeting them and would like to keep communications open for the future. (Again, see the next chapter for details on how to handle—and encourage—multiple job offers.)

22.
Multiple Interviews, Multiple Offers

False optimism and laziness lead many job-hunters to be content with only one interview in process at any given time. That severely reduces the odds of landing the best job in town within your chosen timeframe. Complacency guarantees that you will continue to operate in a buyer's market.

The recommended approach is to generate as many interviews as possible in a two- to three-week period. Interviewing skills are learned and consequently improve with practice. With the improved skills comes a greater confidence, and those natural interview nerves disperse. Your confidence shows through to potential employers, and you are perceived in a positive light. And because other companies are interested in you, everyone will move more quickly to secure your services. That is especially important if you are unfortunate enough to be unemployed. Being out of work is when you need money the most and is the time when the salary you can command on the open market is substantially reduced. The interview activity you generate will help offset this.

By generating multiple interviews, you bring the time of the first job offer closer and closer. That one job offer can be quickly parlayed into a number of others. And with a single job offer, your unemployed status has, to all intents and purposes, passed.

Immediately, you can call every company with whom you've met, and explain the situation. "Mr. Johnson, I'm calling because while still under consideration with your company I have received a job offer from one of your competitors. I would hate to make a decision without the chance of speaking with you again. I was very impressed by my meeting with you. Can we get together in the next couple of days?" End, of course, with a question that carries the conversation forward.

If you were in the running at all, your call will usually generate another interview; Mr. Johnson does not want to miss out on a suddenly prized commodity. Remember: It is human nature to want the very things one is about to lose. So you see, your simple offer can be multiplied almost by the number of interviews you have in process at the time.

A single job offer can also be used to generate interviews with new firms. It is as simple as making your usual telephone networking presentation, but ending it differently. You would be very interested in meeting with them because of your knowledge of the company/product/service, but also because you have just received a job offer—would it be possible to get together in the next couple of days?

Relying on one interview at a time can only lead to prolonged anxiety, disappointment, and possibly unemployment. That reliance is due to the combination of false optimism, laziness, and fear of rejection. Those are traits that cannot be tolerated except by confirmed defeatists, for defeat is the inevitable result of those traits. As Heraclitus said, "Character is destiny." Headhunters say, "The job offer that cannot fail will."

Self-esteem, on the other hand, is vital to your success, and happiness is found with it. And with it you will begin to awake each day with a vitality previously unknown. Vigor will increase, your enthusiasm will rise, and desire to achieve will burn within. The more you do today, the better you will feel tomorrow.

Even when you follow this plan to the letter, not every interview will result in an offer. But with many irons in the fire, an occasional firm "no" should not affect your morale. It won't be the first or last time you face rejection. Be persistent, and above all, close your mind to all negative and discouraging influences. The success you experience from implementing this plan will increase your store of willpower and determination, effect the successful outcome of your job hunt, and enrich your whole life. Start today.

The key to your success is preparation. Remember, it is necessary to plan and organize in order to succeed. Failing is easy—it requires no effort. It is the achievement of success that requires effort; and that means effort today, not tomorrow, for tomorrow never comes. So start building that well-stocked briefcase today.

Conclusion:
The Glittering Prizes

It's time for action, to wrestle job offers from the other contenders at the job interview. All victories have their foundation in careful preparation, and in finishing *Knock 'em Dead*, you are loaded for bear and ready for the hunt.

Your winning attitude is positive and active—dream jobs don't come to those who sit and wait—and you realize that success depends on getting out and generating interviews for yourself. At those interviews, you will maintain the interviewer's interest and attention by carrying your half of the conversation. What you ask will show your interest, demonstrate your analytical abilities, and carry the conversation forward. If in doubt about the meaning of a question, you will ask one of your own to clarify it.

The corporate body recognizes that its most valuable resource is in those employees who understand and contribute towards its goals. These people have something in common: They all recognize their differing jobs as a series of challenges and problems, each to be anticipated, met, and solved. It's that attitude that lands jobs and enhances careers.

People with that attitude advance their careers faster than others, because they possess a critical awareness of universally-admired business practices and value systems. They then leverage their careers by projecting the personality traits that most closely complement those practices and values.

As I said at the beginning of this book, a job interview is a ritualized mating dance. The name of that dance is "attitude." Now that you know the steps, you are ready to whirl away with the glittering prizes. There is no more to say except go to your next interview and knock 'em dead.

Appendices

How Do I Choose a Headhunter?

Choose a headhunter with the same care and attention you would choose a spouse or an accountant. This person is more than just a conduit to that next job—if you choose prudently he or she can become a lifetime consultant able to guide you step by step up the ladder of success.

First of all, understand that there are different types of permanent employment services:

- employment agencies where you pay the fee;
- employment agencies where the employer pays the fee;
- contingency and retained search firms.

Those are the three broad categorizations. Their services are all essentially the same in that they will represent you to employers with whom they have existing requisitions.

A small segment of the industry charges you to get a job. To avoid surprises, you will want to determine with which type of company you are doing business. Fortunately, the majority of employment service companies today charge the employer, not you.

All except the retained group will also represent you to existing clients with whom they do not have a requisition but do have a relationship. Only employment agencies will actively market you to a large number of companies with whom they may or may not have an existing relationship.

So what type of company is best for you? Quite simply, the one that will get you the right job offer. The problem is that there are thousands of companies in each of these broad categories, which makes it difficult to sort the good from the bad.

Let's explode one or two myths. A retained executive-search firm (one that gets paid by the client, regardless of the outcome of the search) is not necessarily any better, or more professional, than a contingency-search firm (one that only expects payment on successful completion of a search), which in turn is not necessarily better or more professional than a regular employment agency. Each has its exemplary practitioners and its charlatans. Your goal is to avoid the charlatans and get representation by an exemplary outfit.

Make the choice carefully, and having made the choice, stick with it and listen to the advice you are given. Here are some selection guidelines.

- A company's involvement in professional associations is always a good sign. It demonstrates commitment and a level of competence. In the employment-services industry, the National Association of Personnel Consultants (NAPC) is one of the key professional organizations, with state associations in all 50 states. The National Association of Corporate Personnel Recruiters (NACPR) is another.

- Involvement in independent or franchise networks of firms can also be a powerful plus. For example, an independent network like the National Personnel Associates group has more than 300 member firms around the continental United States and Europe. Membership in one of the leading franchise groups is also positive. These networks also have extensive training programs that help assure a high caliber of consultant. They can be especially helpful if you are looking to change jobs and move across the country (or further) at the same time. Many of the independent and franchise network members also belong to the NAPC.

- Ask whether your contact has a CPC designation. CPC and its international equivalent CIPC stand for Certified Personnel Consultant and Certified International Personnel Consultant, respectively. A CIPC designation requires that the holder already have a CPC designation, and requires adherence to an international code of ethics as designated by the International Personnel Services Association (IPSA). The CPC and new CIPC designations are recognized as a standard of excellence and commitment only achieved after rigorous training and study. Although certification may be applied for after two years' experience in the personnel consulting business, the studying involved usually means that even the newest holders of a CPC have five years' experience, while the average CPC probably has seven to ten years' experience and contacts under his or her belt. Qualified CPCs can also be relied upon to have superior knowledge of the legalities and ethics of the recruitment and hiring process, along with the expertise and tricks of the trade that only come from years of hands-on experience—all of which can be put to work on your behalf.

It's good sense to have a friend in the business with an ear to the ground on your behalf as you continue your climb up the corporate ladder. So find an NAPC member in good standing with a CPC designation, and listen to what he or she tells you. A listing of all current CPC designates who are also members of NAPC is available in the *National Directory of Personnel Consultants by Specialization*, published by NAPC in Alexandria, VA.

What If I Am Asked to Take a Drug Test?

"Would you be willing to take a drug test as a condition of employment?"

Rightly or wrongly, drug testing as a condition of employment is much more common than in years past; it is likely to remain part of the job-search landscape for the foreseeable future. We can reasonably expect that by the mid-nineties, up to one out of every three jobs will require some form of drug testing as part of the selection process.

The Supreme Court has upheld drug testing programs for federal employees holding law enforcement positions, and for customs personnel involved in drug interdiction activities. While there is no direct link between these governmental policies and private industry hiring, the rulings have been interpreted as reflecting our society's general acceptance of drug testing. Recently, Senator Orrin Hatch introduced Senate legislation designed to promote private-sector testing; interestingly, one of the main planks of the proposed bill was a call for national accuracy standards. (The significance of this provision will become clearer later on in this section.)

Recently, the U.S. Chamber of Commerce estimated that half of all Fortune 500 companies engage in some form of drug testing, either in the selection process or as part of random testing programs subsequent to hiring. As it turns out, the vast majority of testing is done to screen potential employees; the Employment Management Association has concluded that once hired, you are less likely to be subjected to drug testing than you were as an applicant (unless, of course, you exhibit signs of drug abuse on the job).

Perhaps you are reading this section out of curiosity, because drugs and drug testing are in the news these days. You may even think to yourself, "Well, this is all very interesting, but *I* don't take drugs; none of this applies to me." Unfortunately, you couldn't be more wrong.

Drug testing is everyone's business, because even those who have no problem with abusing controlled substances can be maligned by a false reading on a drug test. Such readings are, alas, all too common. Drug testing as it is practiced in today's workplace is rife with false positives, or, stated somewhat less clinically, mistakes. These mistakes provide seemingly authoritative "evidence" that you use illicit drugs when you do not.

What causes false positives? There are a number of factors, but of greatest interest here is the way many everyday foods, liquids, and over-the-counter drugs can set off alarms meant to identify serious drug abuse. By taking a pain reliever that contains ibuprofen, for instance—as millions do for relief of any number of aches and pains—you are increasing the risk that you will test positive for marijuana use. If you suffer from a cold and want to be sure to get the sleep necessary to put in a good day at work tomorrow, you may decide to take a nighttime cold medication; but if there is a surprise drug test the next day, you may learn to your surprise that you are an abuser of amphetamines!

False positives can occur as the result of asthma medications you receive on prescription, or because of cross-reacting chemicals in that doctor-prescribed and controlled diet plan. Has your physician instructed you to take the sedative valium? If you do, a drug test could earn you a reputation as an angel dust fan. You are likely to show up as a morphine addict if you've suffered a bad cold or cough and have been prescribed codeine or certain other medications. This may also happen if you indulge in that most wicked of all addictions: lust for poppy seed bagels. That's what two bagel-hefting Navy doctors discovered recently: their careers nearly ran aground when two consecutive tests branded them as users of morphine. A few weeks later, however, the Navy discovered the error and traced it to the ship's commissary. The consumption levels of the bagels in question, the Navy eventually admitted, were well within the range of "normal dietary use."

The pharmaceutical companies that sell the tests list the *known* substances that are *proven* to cross react, but that doesn't mean that those administering the tests can always be depended upon to possess this information or use it wisely. It should be noted, too, that the test manufacturers admit the tests are sometimes just plain wrong, poppy seeds or no poppy seeds; currently, the line is that urinalysis carries no more than a five percent inaccuracy rate. (This is misleading, however, as we shall see.)

Five percent doesn't seem like much, does it? Many businesses and organizations seem to have deemed that error rate to be an acceptable level of risk. Stop for a moment, though, and ask yourself this: what happens if you are the unlucky one out of twenty wrongly identified as a drug abuser? Remember, the mere presence of a positive on your test is usually enough to brand you as a person with a drug problem. By contrast, a breathalyzer test for alcohol is designed to determine whether you have consumed *too much* liquor. Drug testing recognizes no such niceties: if the buzzer goes off, you're one of the bad guys.

A little background is probably in order here. Drug testing recognizes (or, at any rate, is meant to recognize) whether miniscule traces of a certain substance are present in the urine. While marijuana, which accounts for over 90% of all positive findings, stays in an average-sized body for about three weeks, the length of time any substance stays in your system is affected by your actual body weight.

Now then. Since the question is not whether you *decided* to put a substance in your body, but whether it is *present*, an interesting set of issues arises. We are all well aware of the ongoing conflict over second-hand cigarette smoke; current evidence indicates that even those who don't smoke tobacco can, if they breathe air polluted by cigarette smoke, suffer adverse health effects as a result. The smoke still enters the body, even if you don't have a cigarette between your lips. Well, marijuana makes smoke, too. And you don't have to smoke it for it to show up in your system; just go to a party where someone else is smoking it, or sit next to a puffing Wall Streeter at a Grateful Dead concert, and you could have your professional reputation destroyed by an "accurate" drug test the next day!

What's more, the five percent accuracy rate claimed by the manufacturers of urinalysis tests is, while true in the strict sense, not meaningful in practical terms. In clinical testing conditions, these tests have indeed been shown to perform at or under five percent where errors are concerned. But your drug test will not be conducted in clinical testing conditions. It will be conducted "in the field"—out in the real world, where things aren't monitored quite so closely. When the lab's emphasis is on weeding out drug users (rather than on research), the error rate can be expected to balloon to fourteen percent, according to estimates made in the Journal of Analytic Toxicology.

But why should we rely on estimates? The Center for Disease Control (CDC) and the National Institute on Drug Abuse (NIDA) ran a nine-year study on the accuracy of private sector laboratories. Private sector labs, where your specimen is most likely to be handled, hardly inspire confidence: they don't have to be licensed, they usually operate under no legislated employee training requirements, and they are often staffed by workers receiving only minimum wage. The results of the study? Brace yourself.

When the labs knew the specimens in question came from the CDC and the NIDA, the results were extremely impressive, and could serve as a model for any testing program. But when the labs did not know who the specimens were coming from—when the specimen, in other words, could have been yours—a very different picture emerged. Up to sixty-six out of a hundred samples showed false positives. That translates to two-thirds of a given group of people having their reputations and careers destroyed for no particular reason. At the same time, the inaccuracy rate for screening known abusers under these "blind" conditions was shown to rise to as high as 100%! Translation: the labs gave a clean bill of health to up to 100% of the sample specimens *known* to contain traces of illegal drugs.

It's quite clear, then, that the claims of the pharmaceutical industry notwithstanding, there is cause for considerable concern when it comes to accuracy in urinalysis testing. In theory, the numbers may border on acceptable (though they are not iron-clad by any means); in practice, however, the record is horrendous.

What causes the inaccuracy? First of all, juggling urine specimens all day long is not exactly everyone's idea of ultimate career fulfillment; it is not surprising that the quality of work is less than exemplary. Second, urine testing is easy to do incorrectly. The specimens go stale quickly and react poorly to extremes of heat and cold. In addition, urine that is too acidic or too alkaline can skew the test results; these problems can be caused simply by the subject's eating spicy foods.

Bearing all of this depressing news in mind, then, how are you supposed to answer when asked whether you would submit to a drug test?

If you want the job offer—and at this stage of the game the offer is all that's important—your short answer is "Yes." There is nothing at all wrong with answering in this way and using whatever offer may arise to negotiate with other employers, as outlined elsewhere in this book. Remember that being asked *whether* you would take a test is not the same thing as being asked *when* you would take a test. Initially, the question is invariably placed on a hypothetical footing: "Would you have any problem with taking a drug test?" And once you assent to the testing, you have about a fifty-fifty chance of making it through without actually being asked to provide a specimen.

When it appears that the drug test is about to move from the hypothetical into the realm of stark reality, though, you will need to protect yourself. Your good reputation could be in jeopardy.

Prior to the testing, an ethical company will give you a form to read, fill in, and sign. This formalizes your permission to conduct the test, and affirms your willingness to comply with company policies on the matter. The form should also list all the over-the-counter and prescription drugs—and other ingestible substances—known to cross-react with the test that will be used. Be sure to indicate on the form any of these substances and *all* drugs and medications you have taken recently. (The form often asks you to note what has been taken "within the week," but you should also list any medications you have taken in the past few weeks. Depending on your body weight, one week may not be enough to flush the residues from your system.)

Do not fail to note *every* applicable item! Five minutes ago you had no idea that a bagel or a cold medication could earn you a reputation as a lowlife; nothing is "innocent" when it comes to cross reaction with drug tests. And all tests cross react with something!

If the above mentioned ethical courtesies are not extended to you prior to the test, cover yourself by saying something along the following lines.

> "Yes, I would of course be willing to take a drug test as part of the condition of employment. However, I have seen some reliable reporting that says many of these tests could show me to be a drug abuser if I have taken something as innocuous as a headache pill. I have been assured that you will not take offense if I ask what medications the test is known to cross react with."

Again, if you are provided with the list, you should add whatever medications you have been taking, whether or not they appear on the list. If the company is unable or unwilling to give you the list you will be faced with a judgment call. Only you can say how important your good name is. In this case, you might ask if, under the circumstances, the company would be willing to have your personal physician administer the test.

If the test should show a positive result, ethical organizations will agree to guarantee you a backup test *of another type* because of the chance of a false reading. Reputable pharmaceutical companies and laboratories recommend an additional test upon the first occurrence of a positive; you are well within your rights to ask if you will be given this basic consideration. If the company in question refuses to offer you a backup test, there is a good chance it is because they are costly and the company is short-sighted enough to want to scrimp in this area. It is your decision whether or not to interview or work at such a firm.

There is, unfortunately, more bad news you should be aware of when it comes to corporate drug testing policies. A number of companies have shown themselves to be less than ethical in their handling of samples received as a result of drug testing; people have unwittingly been tested for asthma, diabetes, epilepsy, and even pregnancy. Check the form carefully before signing it, and if there appear to be loopholes you'd rather see closed, point them out.

Suppose that somewhere during the process, someone at the firm comments suspiciously that you seem remarkably well briefed on this topic. You might reply along these lines.

> "Yes, I am; this is because I realize that there is only one thing more important to a professional than his or her competence, and that is reputation. Being a person who is attentive to detail and proud of it, I took the time to research this issue thoroughly."

Your demeanor is all-important; if you act like you have something to hide, people will assume that you do. Stay calm, and express your concerns from a position of self-assured professionalism.

So much for the preliminaries. We move now to the question of what to do if you have decided it is in your best interests to take a drug test. If you are, rightly or wrongly, identified as a drug user, there will be three pertinent questions to answer.

- Will word reach your colleagues in the professional community, and if so, when?

- Will word reach your neighborhood, and if so, when?

- If you are branded as a drug abuser, just how long will it take you to get another job?

They aren't pleasant questions to have to answer; my feeling is that you should give yourself every advantage before the test, so that you will reduce your chances of ever having to face these quandaries. I am not saying you should "cheat"; as we have seen, the problem is not so much people cheating on drug tests as drug tests cheating innocent people out of rightful opportunity. You should, in my view, do everything in your power to avoid being placed in a compromising position. Following are suggestions of some things you can do to put the odds in your favor before you take the test.

The moment you learn that you may have to take a test, your objective should be to flush your body out. Drink lots and lots of water; seize every opportunity to void yourself the day of the test. If you can, schedule the test for after work; claim that it is impossible for you to get away in the morning. The most concentrated urine specimens are those generated first thing in the morning; those given later in the afternoon are less potent.

You will want to make use of as many diuretics (items that promote urination) as you can work into your diet. Coffee, tea, and juices are excellent diuretics; so is beer, but you should not drink alcohol prior to an interview, for reasons I have outlined elsewhere in this book.

Jogging or working out makes you sweat, which helps clean out the system. Exercise also improves alertness and physical agility. (Anyone in pursuit of a new job should exercise on a regular basis, anyway.)

Saunas and steam baths will help remove impurities from your system, as well as increase your need to consume liquids. What's more, they are relaxing, rejuvenating, and good for the skin.

Finally, you may want to pick up a bottle of B-complex vitamins and take some for the few days preceding your test date. They are good for you, of course, and will leave all sorts or wholesome stuff in your specimen, but they will also give the little glass jar you pass in a healthy yellow glow that fairly shouts: "This one is no crack addict!" (Well, appearances do count for something.)

□ □ □

Remember, in the early stages, your goal is to generate offers; you want people bidding for your services. Even an offer you don't want can be leveraged into another and better offer elsewhere. Once you know you want to work at a given company, you will have to decide for yourself if it is worth undergoing the rigors and uncertainties of drug testing to obtain a job there. Many people decide that it is, and for reasons that are perfectly valid for them. I would suggest, though, that you bear in mind that potential employers are on their best behavior when wooing new recruits; if you have to go through all of this prior to the wedding, what sort of marriage is it likely to be?

By the way, if you do decide *against* working for a company that insists on drug testing, you might consider writing the higher-ups in the firm to tell them—politely—the reasons underlying your decision. Many of these executives have no idea how difficult or degrading undergoing a drug test can be. An argument can certainly be made that they should be exposed to the concerns of the people whose lives their decisions affect; too often, company policies are established in an insulated environment that does not take basic human sensibilities into account.

Corporate America is currently wringing its collective hands over the perceived fickleness and lack of loyalty in today's work force; but those in authority really should not be surprised if this is the case. Loyalty is a two-way street; today, employees and potential employees are sometimes so casually assumed to be guilty before proven innocent that they cannot be faulted for seeking to make a contribution elsewhere.

What Should I Know about Smoking and the Work Place?

"Are you a smoker?" "Do you have any problem working in a smoke-free environment?"

If you are one of the 50 million Americans who smoke, you probably don't need this book to tell you that times have changed.

The non-smoking camp has definitely moved into the ascendancy over the last decade and a half. The American Society for Personnel Administration tells us that 60% of all companies enforce some smoking restrictions; many of them ban smoking in the work place altogether.

Study after study has made it clear that smokers simply cost companies more than non-smokers. Most managers (including, quite possibly, the ones who interview you) are familiar with the "butt break" problem: an employee who incorporates two or three more breaks over the course of a day than one who doesn't is, in effect, leaving work twenty to thirty minutes early, day after day. In addition to issues of productivity, there are health care costs to be considered: a recent Control Data Corporation study estimated the additional insurance costs for a smoker as compared to a non-smoker as something on the order of eighteen percent. There are other expenses, some both dramatic and unexpected: one company reduced its office cleaning bill by $6,000 a month when they went smoke-free.

If you smoke, you will almost certainly be in the minority where you work. And if you want to smoke on the job, you should expect to be in for a disappointment. Although Oregon has adopted (and a handful of other states are considering) laws that protect a smoker's right to work, the job hunter who smokes will be fighting an uphill battle. This is one area where discrimination is totally accepted (and, the nonsmoking lobby would say, acceptable). You can expect your interviewers to be nonsmokers, and you can expect them to take a dim view of your habit. In addition to affecting your ability to land job offers, smoking will probably make it more difficult for you to be accepted by co-workers, work well with supervisors, and attract promotions.

It's unlikely anyone will come out and say, "Gee, Sam, we'd like to hire you, but we don't like smokers." You may even be lucky enough not to have the subject come up during the interview. But if you expect your status not to affect your candidacy, you're wrong. That invisible ashtray halo will hang around you, and it is, to put it plainly, offensive to nonsmokers. In a close decision, it is likely to tip the balance against you, and you should be aware of that.

For the Nonsmoker

As a nonsmoker, you have a right to a smoke-free workplace. People who choose not to smoke, but are forced to work in the presence of those who do smoke on the job, become passive smokers—and passive smokers open themselves to the possibility of health problems.

Fortunately, your sense of smell will tell you if you are about to join a company where people smoke. The difficult question comes when you find the company you really want to work for, but learn that everyone there puffs like a brickworks smokestack: what do you do?

As important as what to do is when to do it. There is little to be gained by bringing up your concerns before you get a firm offer. Remember that you are at the interview to get the job offer, and while you don't have to accept it, you have nothing without it. By using the leveraging techniques outlined earlier in this book, you can generate other interviews with other companies, and may come across a firm that excites you even more.

If you do decide to join a team that features among its members those who smoke in the work place, you must proceed cautiously. People who smoke are fighting a rear guard action, not only at work, but in virtually every other area of their lives. These days, everyone seems to mind if they smoke, and this can include family, business associates, spouses—you name it. Many smokers develop defensive or even hostile reactions to those who are perceived as challenging their "territorial rights," and can be expected to battle for every square inch. Moreover, some who still smoke on the job do so because they can: they are in positions of authority, and have seen to it that the standards of "the good old days" still obtain. You don't want to give them an excuse to paint you as an enemy, especially early on.

When you have a firm offer in hand, discuss the matter with another nonsmoker at the company. *Do not* accept the offer until you have learned what that person has done to get by, and whether the same techniques will work for you. Try to determine where you will work, with whom, and under what general conditions. If you don't address these issues now, it could be more difficult once you are on board.

Of course, you may well make contact with other nonsmokers who are prepared to make a stand on the issue—but is this really the way you want to start the job? If you join an organization that lacks a smoke-free rule, you should probably be prepared to suffer quietly for awhile. You will be an unproven commodity; speaking up too soon could jeopardize your chances of fitting in and steaming ahead with your career.

Just being quiet, however, doesn't mean that you aren't working on the problem. There are a number of things you can do.

- Identify other nonsmokers who obviously object to smoking. These are the people who move away from someone who lights up a cigarette, who cough and rub their eyes when smokers are around, who wave the smoke away from in front of their faces, and so on.

- As you identify your allies, show empathy with them. Perhaps the next time the smoker lights up in the office and the nonsmoker coughs, you can say quietly that you know how it feels because smoke bothers you too.

- Gather relevant clippings, pamphlets and articles for later use. When the time is right, and you have an established place within the organization, you can start voicing your concerns and back them up with facts your employer will listen to.

Gathering the information should be fairly easy; as we've noted, the tide is definitely turning against smokers these days. Following are some "fast facts" you can eventually use to bolster your case.

- *The Environmental Protection Agency* has identified tobacco smoke as "a major source of indoor pollution."

- *The American Society of Personnel Administration* has found that the majority of American companies—over 60%—already restrict smoking.

- *The Smoking Policy Institute* has found that 24% of all American companies now ban smoking entirely in the work place, and that that number is increasing.

- *Control Data Corporation* has found that nonsmoking employees have insurance claims 18% lower than those of smokers.

- *The Office of Technology Assessment* has estimated that smoking costs American businesses over $65 billion yearly in health-related costs, including time off work due to smoking-related health problems.

Late Update: Beat the Psychological Tests!

In late 1989, Congress banned most private sector applications of the polygraph test, voice stress analysis, and other electronic screening methods. While many government personnel (for instance, those involved in drug interdiction activities) are still subject to these tests, many private employers have had to change their ways, and are increasingly turning to psychological testing to weed out what they consider to be undesirable job applicants. These tests may be known as aptitude tests, personality profiles, or by other names, but in the end they are all the same thing: the next best thing to the old, now-illegal methods for finding out if you show signs of being a "risky" hire.

Actually, though the 1989 legislation has led to new popularity for the psychological tests, they have been around for decades. Psychological exams come in two flavors: one is a face-to-face meeting with a psychologist, and the other (far more common) is a written test, often multiple choice.

In any discussion of this issue, we should bear in mind that psychology is, by the admission of even its own practitioners, an inexact science. It cannot yield any definitive litmus test on your potential employability. Yet many companies are pretending that it can, and are grafting the imprecise discipline of psychological testing onto the equally imprecise one of employment selection. The result is an essentially insight-free mess that is, nevertheless, easy to administer, relatively cheap, and increasingly popular. Those seeking employment are often asked to answer "a few routine questions" that end up being anything but routine. The tests, which are (in theory) not to be used as the sole basis for a hiring decision, can nevertheless have a huge effect on peoples' livelihoods.

The whole concept of psychological testing is fraught with controversy. Some view the tests as an intrusion into private life, and with good reason: they often ask blatantly illegal questions about, say, your religious beliefs. Others request information about your sexuality, and many of these queries are illegal in states that have adopted legislation protecting freedom of sexual preference. Laws or no laws, however, there the questions are, in black and white. If you refuse to take a test that is a "required" part of the selection process, you will almost certainly be denied employment. (Not surprisingly, several court cases have been initiated by disgruntled applicants.)

It isn't surprising that many of the companies using the tests are concerned about the potential honesty of prospective employees. Each year American industry loses an estimated $40 billion from employee theft. But while honesty is often one of the behavioral profiles examined, the tests tend to emphasize the examination of aptitude and suitability. Often, the exams are geared to evaluating the amount of energy a person might bring to the job, how he or she would handle stress, and what attitude toward job, peers, and management would be likely to be prevalent.

Unfortunately, answering a psychological test with complete personal honesty may very well threaten your chance of being offered employment. That's the bad news. Here's the good news: you can beat the tests without having to compromise your personal integrity.

Not long ago I did an in-house employee selection and motivation seminar for a large corporation; I was asked for my opinion on the subject of psychological testing. I replied that the tests were often used inappropriately as a pass/fail criterion for hiring, and that anyone with half a mind could come up with the desired or correct answers. "The question is," I concluded, "how many people who could have served you well will you miss out on because of a test?"

The managers assured me that they had a test in use that was "virtually infallible" in helping to identify strong hires, and certainly not subject to the machinations of the average applicant. They asked if I would be prepared to take it. I not only agreed, but also promised to prove my point. "Let me take the test twice," I said. "The first profile you get will tell you to hire me; the second will say I'm a bad risk."

I took the test twice that day. "Applicant #1" came back with a strong recommendation for hire. "Applicant #2" came back with a warning to exercise caution before considering taking him on.

How was this possible? Well, there is something the tests ignore: none of us is the same person in the workplace as in our personal life. Over a period of time at work, we come to understand the need for different behavioral patterns and different ways of interacting with people.

Sometimes our more considered, analytical, logical approaches pass over from our "professional self" into the personal realm. However, in the world of work, we are not expected to try to override the "corporate way" of doing things with our personal preferences. When this happens, and personal preferences take precedence over existing corporate theories of behavior, we get warnings and terminations. In other words, as professionals we are inculcated with a set of behavioral patterns that are supplied to us over the years to enable us to be successful and productive for our employers.

Did I really "fool" the test? No. I was completely honest both times. The "winning" test was the one in which I viewed myself—and, thus, described myself—as the thoroughly professional white-collar worker in the job for which I was applying. The "losing" test was the one I used to describe myself as the kind of person I see myself in my personal life.

This was not a hoax perpetrated by a smart aleck. I am that person they would have hired, and I possess a strong track record to back up my claim. I learned the behaviors necessary to succeed, adopted them, and made them my own—just as you have undoubtedly done.

Many of the tests simply lack an awareness of the complexity of the human mind. They seem to miss the point when they ask us to speak honestly about our feelings and beliefs. They do not take into account that our learned behaviors in our professional lives are, invariably, quite distinct from the behaviors we accept in our personal lives.

The secret of my success—and of yours, if you must take a psychological test—is really quite simple.

How to Prepare For, Read, and Answer the Tests

Born independently wealthy, very few of us would be doing the jobs we do. But we *are* doing them, and we have learned certain sets of skills and behavioral traits that are critical to our ability to survive and succeed professionally. The first thing you must do, then, is identify and separate the professional you from the personal you.

☐ **Step One: Never consider answering a test from the viewpoint of your innermost beliefs.** Instead, use your learned and developed professional behavior traits and modus operandi. Ask yourself, "How has my experience as a professional _____ taught me to think and respond to this?"

To do this effectively (and to understand ourselves a little better in the process), we need some further insights into the three critical skill sets that every professional relies on to succeed.

- Professional/technical skills (whether you're a secretary or a senior vice president).

- Industry skills (such as—if you happen to be in banking— your overall knowledge of the world of banking: how things work, how things get done, what is accepted within the industry, and so on).

- Professional behavior traits (the traits discussed in Chapter 12 of this book that all employers look for, and that will get you ahead once you are on the job).

☐ **Step Two: Look at yourself from the employer's point of view.** (Review "The Other Side of the Desk" for some helpful ideas.) Evaluate what traits come into play that enable you to discharge your duties effectively. Examine the typical crises/emergencies that are likely to arise: what supportive behavioral traits are necessary to overcome them? As you do this, you will almost certainly relive some episodes that seemed to put you at a disadvantage for a time. When it was tough to do things the right way, you had to buckle down and see the problem through, even though doing so did not necessarily "come naturally." The fact is, though, you overcame the obstacle. Remember *how* you did so, and keep that in mind as you answer the questions.

Conversely, you will want to look at those instances where a crisis had a less than successful outcome. What traits did you swear you would develop and use for next time?

Highlighting such traits simply constitutes your acknowledgment of the supremacy of learned behavior in the workplace. It does *not* constitute lying. (Why do you think so many professionals strive to keep their business lives separate from their personal lives? What is the point of such a separation if the two lives are identical?)

☐ **Step Three: Think of people you've known who have failed on the job.** Why did they fail? What have you learned from their mistakes and make a part of the "professional you"?

☐ **Step Four: Think of people you've known who have succeeded on the job.** Why did they succeed? What have you learned from their success and made a part of the "professional you"?

Once you have completed this exercise in detail, you will have effectively determined how a professional _____ would react in a wide range of circumstances, and identified the ways in which you have, over time, developed a "professional self" to match that profile.

Getting Ready for the Test

Any test can be nerve-racking, but when it comes to psych tests your livelihood is in the balance. Desperate times, of course, call for desperate measures. Accordingly, you should be sure, as you enter the testing area, that you are armed with the ultimate failsafe. If at all possible, carry with you the one object that will guarantee you the chance to make the best possible impression as you take the test: a cup of coffee. (Yes, I am serious; the reasoning here will become clear very soon.)

The tests instruct you to answer quickly, offering the first response that comes to mind. Don't. Following this path may well cost you a job. Instead, look at the test in terms of the exercises outlined above; provide reasoned responses from the viewpoint of the "professional you."

Time limits are usually not imposed; on the contrary, those administering the test will often begin the proceedings with a soothing "Take your time, there's no pressure." (Except, of course, the minor pressure of knowing a job offer is on the line!)

In a face-to-face meeting with a psychologist, use the same techniques we have discussed throughout *Knock 'em Dead* to qualify the questions before answering them; when you suspect a trap, employ the tricks that will help you clarify things and buy time.

Beware: the written tests may contain "double blinds," where you are asked a question on page one, and then asked a virtually identical one thirty or forty questions later. The technique is based on the belief that most of us can tell a lie, but few of us can remember that lie under stress, and are therefore likely to answer differently later. This is held to show the potential for untruthfulness. The problem isn't that one answer is likely to deny you employment; the questions are asked in patterns to evaluate your behavior and attitudes on different topics.

So: read the test through before you start answering questions! (There's "plenty of time" and "no pressure," remember?) Review the material at least three times, mentally flagging the questions that seem similar. This way you will be assured of consistency.

Of course, you are likely to encounter ethics questions. "Have you ever stolen anything?" "Have you ever felt guilty?" "Have you ever told a lie?" Avoid the temptation to respond impulsively with something like "Lies? No, I prefer to chop down the damned cherry tree." The truth is we have all done these things in our lives. When you are asked, for instance, if there is anything you would ever change about yourself, or whether you think everyone is dishonest to some degree, the overwhelming likelihood is that your own honesty is being tested: the best answer is probably yes.

If you must address ethics matters in a face-to-face encounter, you can explain your answer, placing it far in the past where appropriate, and explain what you learned from the experience. If such questions must be answered on paper, the best approach is to follow the dictates of your own conscience and try to bring the issue up after the test. You might say something like this:

> "Gee, that question about lying was a tough one. I guess everyone has told a lie at some time in the past, and I wanted to be truthful, so I said yes. But I'd be lying if I didn't tell you it made me nervous. You know, I saw a show on television recently about these tests. It told the story of someone who lost a job because of answering a question just like that; the profile came back with an untrustworthy rating."

This should reduce the odds of your being denied the job in the same way. If the test does come back with a question about your honesty, you will have at least sown seeds of doubt about the validity of such a rating in the interviewer's mind. That doubt, and your disarming honesty, might just turn the tables in your favor.

Resist any temptation to project an image of yourself as an interesting person by the answers you select. These tests are not designed to reward eccentricity; think sliced white bread. You are happy at work and home. You enjoy being around people. You don't spend all your evenings watching movies (unless your name is

Siskel or Ebert). You don't spend your weekends with a computer or pursuing other solitary pastimes (unless you are a programmer or an aspiring Trappist monk). You have beliefs, but not too strong. You respect the beliefs of all others, regardless of their age, sex, race, or religion.

When you finish the test, read through your answers a few times; if you don't like one or two, change them. Don't change too many; if you do, you will risk appearing indecisive. However, if you have a lot of changes, just spill your coffee over the test (I told you there was a reason to bring that cup in with you). Throw the test in the trash—near the top, of course, where its condition can be verified— and ask for another copy. Since you will likely have some measure of privacy for taking the test, you can take on the new test with the added benefit of having the old one in front of you. (You don't mind retrieving that slightly sodden document for the sake of your career, do you?)

All of what I have said here takes for granted that the overriding goal of the employer is to determine whether or not you are suitable for the job. If you can give an accurate affirmative answer to that question, then the approach you take in doing so is—to my way of thinking, anyway—of little consequence. If you have learned and applied what it takes to prosper in your profession, then it is emphatically your right to provide an honest profile of your professional self, in whatever forum you are to be evaluated.

Bibliography

Some of the books listed here may be purchased inexpensively at a bookstore. Most, however, are expensive, so you will find it cost-effective to go to your local library to use them. Many states have an inter-library lending system, so if the book you want is not available, the librarian can usually get it for you.

As mentioned earlier, you should not rely solely on reference books. Their size and scope often makes them a little out of date, and they aren't all updated or published every year. Ask your librarian for the most recent editions.

Of Special Interest to Readers of This Book:

Resumes that Knock 'em Dead. Bob Adams, Inc., Holbrook, MA. An in-depth look at the principles behind the resumes that really get jobs. Available at most bookstores.

The Instant Resume Writer. Lightning Word, Santa Clara. Software for the PC based on the above book. Available at most software stores.

General Guides and Directories:

Billion Dollar Directory: America's Corporate Families. Dun & Bradstreet: New York, NY. Lists companies alphabetically, geographically, and by product, and charts the various divisions and subdivisions of major corporations.

The National Job Bank. Bob Adams, Inc.: Boston, MA. A comprehensive directory that lists more than 15,000 major employers alphabetically for each state and the District of Columbia. Contains contact information, a description of the business, common positions filled, educational backgrounds sought, and fringe benefits offered. Also provides industrial/geographical cross-index.

Standard & Poor's Register of Corporations, Directors, and Executives. Standard & Poor's/McGraw-Hill: New York, NY. Comes in three volumes. The first lists all major companies by industry and geography; the second gives the details and contact information on those companies; the third gives personal data on many corporate executives.

State Manufacturing Directories. Every state has one. It uses a form similar to the *Standard & Poor's Register.* It usually comes in one volume, has contact data for the various companies, but has no personal information about executives. Repeats some information from the *Standard & Poor's Register,* but also includes many smaller, local companies.

Thomas Register of American Manufacturers. Thomas Publishing Company: New York. An enormous (12-volume) manufacturing business-to-business directory. Thousands of large and small companies in every field.

Other Guides:

Content information for the following directories, and thousands of other reference sources, can be found in the *Directory of Directories* (Gale Research Company: Detroit, MI). Every good library should have one.

Access. National Association of Personnel Consultants: Washington, DC.

Atlanta Job Bank. Bob Adams, Inc.: Holbrook, MA.

Bay Area Employer Directory. James Albin: Sausalito, CA.

Bay Area Employment Agency and Executive Recruiter Directory. James Albin: Sausalito, CA.

Boston Job Bank. Bob Adams, Inc.: Holbrook, MA.

Career Employment Opportunities Directory. Ready Reference Press: Santa Monica, CA.

Career Guide to Professional Associations: A Directory of Organizations by Occupational Field. Carroll Press: Cranston, RI.

*Career Opportunities Index.*Career Research Systems: Huntington Beach, CA.

College Placement Annual. College Placement Council: Bethlehem, PA.

Dallas Job Bank. Bob Adams, Inc.: Holbrook, MA.

Directory of Career Planning and Placement Offices. College Placement Council: Bethlehem, PA.

Directory of Summer Jobs Abroad. Vacation-Work: Oxford, England.

Executive Employment Guide. Management Information Service: New York, NY.

Federal Career Opportunities. Federal Research Service Inc.: Vienna, VA.

Federal Job Information Centers Directory. Office of Personnel Management: Washington, DC.

Federal Jobs. U.S. Government Printing Office: Leesburg, VA.

Greater Chicago Job Bank. Bob Adams, Inc.: Holbrook, MA.

International Jobs: Where They Are, How to Get Them. Addison-Wesley Publishing Company: Reading, MA.

Houston Job Bank. Bob Adams, Inc.: Holbrook, MA.

Job Catalog. Mail Order USA: Washington, DC.

Job Hunter's Guide to 8 Great American Cities. Brattle Publications: Cambridge, MA.

Job Hunter's Guide to the Rocky Mountain West. Brattle Publications: Cambridge, MA.

Job Hunter's Guide to Seattle. Alex Collections: Seattle, WA.

Job Hunter's Guide to the Sunbelt. Brattle Publications: Cambridge, MA.

Los Angeles Job Bank. Bob Adams, Inc.: Holbrook, MA.

Metropolitan New York Job Bank. Bob Adams, Inc.: Holbrook, MA.

Metropolitan Washington (DC) Job Bank. Bob Adams, Inc.: Holbrook, MA.

Multinational Marketing and Employment Directory. World Trade Academy Press: New York, NY.

Ohio Job Bank. Bob Adams, Inc.: Holbrook, MA.

Philadelphia Job Bank. Bob Adams, Inc.: Holbrook, MA.

San Francisco Bay Area Job Bank. Bob Adams, Inc.: Holbrook, MA.

Seasonal Employment. National Park Service, Department of the Interior: Washington, DC.

Seattle Job Bank. Bob Adams, Inc.: Holbrook, MA.

Summer Employment Directory of the United States. Writers Digest Books: Cincinnati, OH.

Summer Jobs: Opportunities in Federal Government. Office of Personnel Management: Washington, DC.

Transactions, Resource Guide to Work, Travel and Study Abroad. Clayton A. Hubbs: Amherst, MA.

Whole World Handbook. Council of International Educational Exchange: New York, NY.

Especially for Women:

AWIS Job Bulletin. Association for Women in Science: Washington, DC.

Blue Collar Jobs for Women. E.P. Dutton Inc.: New York, NY.

Catalyst National Network of Career Resource Centers. Catalyst: New York, NY.

Directory of Career Resources for Women. Ready Reference Press: Santa Monica, CA.

Displaced Homemaker Program Directory. Displaced Homemakers Network: Washington, DC.

Internship Programs for Women. National Society for Internships: Washington, DC.

National Directory of Women's Employment Programs: Who They Are What They Do. Wider Opportunities for Women: Washington, DC.

Professional Women's Groups. American Association of University Women: Washington, DC.

Resource Directory for Affirmative Recruitment in Connecticut. Connecticut Commission of Human Rights: Hartford, CT.

Women Helping Women: A State by State Directory of Services. Women's Action Alliance: New York, NY.

Women's Guide to Career Preparation. Anchor Press (Doubleday): New York, NY.

Women's Guide to Apprenticeship. Women's Bureau, U.S. Department of Labor: Washington, DC.

Especially for Minorities:

Career Development Opportunities for Native Americans. Office of Indian Educational Programs, Bureau of Indian Affairs, Department of the Interior: Washington, DC.

Directory of Career Resources for Minorities. Ready Reference Press: Santa Monica, CA.

Directory of Special Programs for Minority Group Members: Career Information Services, Employment Skills Banks, Financial Aid Services. Garrett Park Press: Garrett Park, MD.

Index to
the Questions

Do you have a degree?
See page **40.**

Do you have any problem working in a smoke-free environment?
See page **211.**

Do you have any questions?
See page **105.**

Do you like regular hours?
See page **154.**

Do you like routine tasks?
See page **154.**

Do you make your opinions known when you disagree with the views of your supervisor?
See page **112.**

Do you pay attention to detail?
See page **124.**

Do you plan to have children?
See page **144.**

Do you prefer working with others or alone?
See page **111.**

Do you think grades should be considered by first employers?
See page **156.**

Do you think people in your profession should be paid more?
See page **182.**

Explain your role as a group/team member.
See page **111.**

Give me an example of a method of working you have used.
See page **121.**

Have you done the best work you are capable of doing?
See page **96.**

Have you ever been asked to resign?
See page **103.**

Have you ever been fired?
See page **102.**

Have you ever been refused a salary increase?
See page **179.**

Have you ever had any financial difficulties?
See page **134.**

How long would you stay with the company?
See page **96.**

How many hours a week do you find it necessary to work to get your job done?
See page **97.**

How many other jobs have you applied for?
See page **104.**

How much are you looking for?
See page **180.**

How much are you making?
See page **39.**

How much do you need to support your family?
See page **179.**

How much do you want?
See page **39.**

How much experience do you have?
See page **41.**

How much will it take to get you?
See page **180.**

How old are you?
See page **143.**

How well do you feel your boss rated your job performance?
See page **110.**

How will you be able to cope with a change in environment?
See page **133.**

How would you define a conducive work atmosphere?
See page **111.**

How would you define your profession?
See page **134.**

How would you evaluate me as an interviewer?
See page **140.**

I'd be interested to hear about some things you learned in school that could be used on the job.
See page **154.**

[Illegal interview questions.]
See page **142.**

I'm not sure you're suitable for the job.
See page **140.**

In hindsight, what have you done that was a little harebrained?
    See page **115.**

In what areas do you feel your supervisor could have done a better job?
    See page **110.**

In what ways has your job changed?
    See page **104.**

In what way is your approach to a challenge different from that of others?
    See page **120.**

In what ways has your job prepared you to take on greater responsibility?
    See page **104.**

In your last job, how did you plan to interview?
    See page **121.**

In your last job, what were some of the things you spent most of your time on, and why?
    See page **103.**

People from your major never work out here. What makes you different?
    See page **154.**

People from your school never work out here. What makes you different?
    See page **154.**

Rate yourself on a scale of one to ten.
    See page **108.**

See this pen I'm holding? Sell it to me.
    See page **133.**

Tell me a story.
    See page **114.**

Tell me about a time when you experienced pressure on the job.
    See page **129.**

Tell me about a time when you put your foot in your mouth.
    See page **136.**

Tell me about an event that really challenged you.
    See page **120.**

Tell me about the last time you felt anger on the job.
    See page **109.**

Tell me about the problems you have living within your means.
    See page **131.**

Tell me about yourself.
    See page **108.**

Tell me how you moved up through the organization.
See page **98**.

Tell me why you have been with one company so long without any appreciable increase in rank or salary.
See page **132**.

Were you ever dismissed from your job for a reason that seemed unjustified?
See page **103**.

What are some of the problems you encounter in doing your job?
See page **138**.

What are some of the things about which you and your supervisor disagreed?
See page **110**.

What are some of the things that bother you?
See page **109**.

What are some of the things you find difficult to do?
See page **138**.

What are some of the things your supervisor did that you disliked?
See page **110**.

What are the broad responsibilities of a _____?
See page **93**.

What are the reasons for your success in this profession
See page **92**.

What are you looking for in your next job?
See page **99**.

What are you making now?
See page **178**.

What are your biggest accomplishments?
See page **97**.

What are your future vocational plans?
See page **153**.

What are your outstanding qualities?
See page **98**.

What are your pet hates?
See page **109**.

What are your qualifications?
See page **97**.

What are your salary requirements?
See page **180**.

What area of your skills/professional development do you want to improve?
See page **132.**

What aspects of your job do you consider most crucial?
See page **94.**

What can you do for us that someone else cannot do?
See page **99.**

What college did you attend, and why did you choose it?
See page **153.**

What did you dislike about your last job?
See page **94.**

What did you like about your last job?
See page **94.**

What difficulties do you have tolerating people with different backgrounds and interests than yours?
See page **115.**

What do you feel is a satisfactory attendance record?
See page **138.**

What do you hope to be earning two to five years from now?
See page **181.**

What do you know about our company?
See page **156.**

What do you think determines progress in a good company?
See page **156.**

What do you think of your current boss?
See page **108.**

What do you think of your last boss?
See page **108.**

What have you done that shows initiative and willingness to work?
See pages **109, 155.**

What have you learned from jobs you have held?
See page **95.**

What have your other jobs taught you?
See page **114.**

What interests you least about this job?
See page **137.**

What interests you most about this job?
See page **99.**

What is an adequate reward for your efforts?
See page **178.**

What is the least relevant job you have held?
See page **95.**

What is the most difficult situation you have faced?
See page **109.**

What is the worst thing you have heard about our company?
See page **133.**

What is your current salary?
See page **178.**

What is your energy level like?
See page **93.**

What is your general impression of your last company?
See page **138.**

What is your greatest strength?
See page **98.**

What is your greatest weakness?
See page **130.**

What is your salary history?
See page **178.**

What kind of decisions are most difficult for you?
See page **131.**

What kind of experience do you have for this job?
See page **93.**

What kind of people do you find it difficult to work with?
See page **139.**

What kind of people do you like to work with?
See page **139.**

What kind of salary are you worth?
See page **181.**

What kind of things do you worry about?
See page **109.**

What makes this job different from your current one?
See page **104.**

What makes this job different from your last one?
See page **104.**

What personal characteristics are necessary for success in your field?
See page **111.**

What qualifications do you have that will make you successful?
See page **155.**

What religion do you practice?
See page **143.**

What type of decisions did you make on your last job?
See page **101.**

What was the last book you read? How did it affect you?
See page **101.**

What was the last movie you saw? How did it affect you?
See page **101.**

What was there about your last company that you didn't particularly like or agree with?
See page **137.**

What was your salary progress on your last job?
See page **178.**

What were some of the minuses on your last job?
See page **139.**

What were you making on your last job?
See page **178.**

What would you do if you had a decision to make and no procedure existed?
See page **122.**

What would you like to be doing five years from now?
See page **96.**

What would you say about a supervisor who was unfair or difficult to work with?
See page **112.**

What would you say if I told you your presentation was lousy?
See page **142.**

What would your references say?
See page **100.**

What's your idea of how industry works?
See page **156.**

When do you expect a promotion?
See page **114.**

When you joined your last company and met the group for the first time, how did you feel?
See page **121.**

Which of the jobs you have held have you liked least?
See page **153.**

Who else have you applied to?
See page **104**.

Why aren't you earning more at your age?
See page **133**.

Why did you leave your last job?
See page **137**.

Why do you feel you are a better _____ than some of your coworkers?
See page **113**.

Why do you think you would like this type of work?
See page **156**.

Why do you want to leave your current job?
See page **137**.

Why do you want to work here?
See page **93**.

Why have you changed jobs so frequently?
See page **136**.

Why should I hire an outsider when I could fill the job with someone inside the company?
See page **134**.

Why should I hire you?
See page **99**.

Why were you fired?
See page **102**.

Why were you out of work for so long?
See page **135**.

With hindsight, how could you have improved your progress?
See page **131**.

Would you be willing to take a drug test as a condition of employment?
See page **203**.

Would you like to have your boss' job?
See page **107**.

Wouldn't you feel better off at another firm?
See page **141**.

You have a doctor's appointment that conflicts with an emergency meeting. What do you do?
See page **113**.

OTHER BOOKS BY MARTIN JOHN YATE
AVAILABLE AT YOUR LOCAL BOOKSTORE

Resumes that Knock 'em Dead

Every single one of the 110 resumes in this book is based on a resume that was successfully used to obtain a job. Many of the resumes included were used to change careers; others resulted in dramatically higher salaries. Some produced both. Yate reviews the marks of a great resume, what type of resume is right for each applicant, what always goes in, what always stays out, and why. Samples of powerful and proven cover letters are also included. 8 1/2 x 11 inches; 216 pages, paperback, $7.95.

Hiring the Best

Contrary to popular belief, not all managers are mystically endowed with the ability to hire the right people. Interviewing is a skill that must be developed, and Martin Yate shows just how to identify the person who provides the best "fit" for any given position. Includes sections on interviewing within the law and hiring clerical help, as well as prewritten interview outlines. 6 x 9 inches; 204 pages, paperback, $9.95.

ALSO OF INTEREST . . .

The Job Bank Series

There are now 17 *Job Bank* books, each providing extensive, up-to-date employment information on hundreds of the largest employers in each job market. Information includes contact person, address to send resumes to, phone number and company description. Most listings include common professional positions, educational backgrounds sought and even fringe benefits offered. Recommended as an excellent place to begin your job search by *The New York Times, The Los Angeles Times, The Boston Globe, The Chicago Tribune,* and many other publications, *Job Bank* books have been used by hundreds of thousands of people to find jobs.

Books available: *The Atlanta Job Bank -- The Boston Job Bank -- The Chicago Job Bank -- The Dallas Job Bank -- The Denver Job Bank -- The Detroit Job Bank -- The Florida Job Bank -- The Houston Job Bank -- The Los Angeles Job Bank -- The Minneapolis Job Bank -- The New York Job Bank -- The Ohio Job Bank -- The Philadelphia Job Bank -- The St. Louis Job Bank -- The San Francisco Job Bank -- The Seattle Job Bank -- The Washington DC Job Bank.* Each book is 6 x 9 inches, over 250 pages, paperback, $12.95.

If you cannot find a book at your local bookstore, you may order it directly from the publisher. Please send payment including $2.75 for shipping and handling (for the entire order) to: Bob Adams, Inc., 260 Center Street, Holbrook, MA 02343. Credit card holders may call 1-800-USA-JOBS (in Massachusetts, 617/767-8100). Please check your local bookstore first.